Spike Milligan was born at Ahmednagar in India in 1918. He received his first education in a tent in the Hyderabad Sindh desert and graduated from there, through a series of Roman Catholic schools in India and England, to the Lewisham Polytechnic. Always something of a playboy, he then plunged into the world of Show Business, seduced by his first stage appearance, at the age of eight, in the nativity play of his Poona convent school. He began his career as a band musician but has since become famous as a humorous scriptwriter and actor in both films and broadcasting. He was one of the main figures in and behind the infamous *Goon Show*. Among the films he has appeared in are *Suspect*, *Invasion*, *Postman's Knock*, *Milligan at Large* and *The Three Musketeers*.

Spike Milligan's published work includes *The Little Potboiler*; *Silly Verse for Kids*; *Dustbin of Milligan*; *A Book of Bits*; *The Bed-Sitting Room* (a play); *The Bald Twit Lion*; *A Book of Milliganimals*; *Puckoon*; *Small Dreams of a Scorpion*; *The Mirror Running* (a book of poetry); *Transports of Delight*; *The Milligan Book of Records, Games, Cartoons and Commercials*; *Badjelly the Witch*; *Dip the Puppy*; *The Spike Milligan Letters* and *More Spike Milligan Letters*, both edited by Norma Farnes; *Open Heart University*; *The Q Annual*; *Unspun Socks from a Chicken's Laundry*; *The 101 Best and Only Limericks of Spike Milligan*; *There's a Lot of It About*; *The Melting Pot*; *Further Transports of Delight*; *Startling Verse for All the Family*; *The Looney: An Irish Fantasy*; *The Lost Goon Shows*; *It Ends with Magic*; *The Bible According to Spike Milligan: The Old Testament*; and *Lady Chatterley's Lover According to Spike Milligan*. With the late Jack Hobbs he also wrote *William McGonagall: The Truth at Last*; *William McGonagall Meets George Gershwin*; and *William McGonagall – Freefall*.

His unique and incomparable seven volumes of war memoirs are: *Adolf Hitler: My Part in His Downfall*; *'Rommel?' 'Gunner Who?'*; *Monty: His Part in My Victory*; *Mussolini: His Part in My Downfall*; *Where Have All the Bullets Gone?*; *Goodbye, Soldier*; and *Peace Work*. To celebrate his seventieth birthday Penguin published a special edition of his first novel *Puckoon*.

Spike Milligan received an honorary CBE in 1992.

Wuthering Heights

According to

Spike Milligan

PENGUIN BOOKS

PENGUIN BOOKS

Published by the Penguin Group
Penguin Books Ltd, 27 Wrights Lane, London W8 5TZ, England
Penguin Books USA Inc., 375 Hudson Street, New York, New York 10014, USA
Penguin Books Australia Ltd, Ringwood, Victoria, Australia
Penguin Books Canada Ltd, 10 Alcorn Avenue, Toronto, Ontario, Canada M4V 3B2
Penguin Books (NZ) Ltd, 182–190 Wairau Road, Auckland 10, New Zealand

Penguin Books Ltd, Registered Offices: Harmondsworth, Middlesex, England

First published by Michael Joseph 1994
Published in Penguin Books 1995
1 3 5 7 9 10 8 6 4 2

The drawings by Balthasar Klossowski de Rola on pages 27, 30 and 57
are reproduced by courtesy of Electra, Milan

Printed in England by Clays Ltd, St Ives plc

Wuthering Heights

According to **S**pike Milligan

Chapter I

801 YEAR OF our Lord and a nit called Lock-wood — i.e. me, the narrator. I have just returned from a visit to my landlord, whereby, killing him has stopped any increase in the rent. In all England, I do not believe I could have fixed on a situation so completely removed from the stir of society; indeed there are societies that do nothing but stir all day. They are porridge brotherhoods, a perfect misanthrope's Heaven: I myself was an imperfect misanthrope as I had piles, and Mr Heathcliff and I are such a suitable pair to divide life's desolation between us, we had half each. A capital fellow, it came to about £40,000. Imagine how my heart warmed to him along with my liver, kidneys and bacon.

'Mr Heathcliff,' I said.

A nod was the answer, but not very loud. 'You are a very tall man,' he said.

'There's a reason,' I said.

'What?' he said.

'I'm on a horse,' I said. 'What are you on?'

'I'm on valium,' he said.

'I am your new tenant, Mr Lockwood.'

'Oh, Christ,' I heard him mutter.

'I hope,' I said, 'I have not inconvenienced you in

soliciting the occupation of Thrushcross Grange.'

'What a creep,' I heard him say. 'Thrushcross Grange is my own, sir,' he said, wincing. He paused, then did a huge wince. He made a foul gesture, and said, 'Come in!' The 'Come in!' was uttered through closed teeth, expressing the sentiment 'Go to the Deuce', so I went to the Deuce, and took tea with him and returned. When Heathcliff saw my horse's breast fairly pushing the chain on the gate, Heathcliff said, 'Look out, your horse's breast is fairly pushing the chain on the gate.' He pulled his hand from his pocket to unchain it. Why he had his hand chained, I'll never know. He opened the gate, then suddenly preceded me up the causeway, breaking wind with every step, my horse getting most of it. As we entered the court he said, 'Ahh, that's better, it was but only for him. Joseph! Take Mr Lockwood's horse; and bring up some wine.'[1]

Joseph was an elderly, nay, an old man, nay, very old, nay *nearly* nay dead old man, nay yet hale and nay hearty.

'The Lord help us!' he soliloquized.

I waited for the Lord to help us, but he didn't. 'Drat it,' said Joseph.

'Drat what?' I said.

He looked at me with displeasure while relieving me of my horse, which relieved itself on him. Looking in my face so sourly, I thought he must be in need of divine aid to digest his dinner (someone like the Virgin Mary and Chips).

Wuthering Heights is Mr Heathcliff's (he was not afraid of heights only widths). Wuthering being descriptive of the tumult to which it is exposed in stormy

[1] Orvieto – thirty shillings a bottle.

weather, pure bracing air giving us the fresh icy north wind and bronchitis. Before entering I paused to admire the carving above the door of griffins and shameless little boys and the name 'Hareton Earnshaw', an active rural paedophile. One step took us into the sitting room, another step we were out of it. They call it here 'the house' because it looks like one. Above the fireplace were several horse pistols used by local horses. The floor was smooth white polished stone, over which I went arse over tip. The furniture would as belong to the northern farmer with, seated in his chair, his mug of ale frothing, the like is to be seen in any circuit of fifteen or sixteen miles among the hills; so if you go at the right time it is open to anybody, after dinner, to walk a fifteen- or sixteen-mile circuit of the hills to find one. Mr Heathcliff is a strange man. He is dark, in dress and manners a gentleman. I think he is Pakistani; his reserve springs from an aversion to showy displays of feeling (though even, as he stood there, he was feeling himself). He would love and hate equally under cover, say, an umbrella or a bus shelter. Mr Heathcliff had reasons for keeping his hand behind him when he meets an acquaintance. It had two thumbs and six fingers.

While encouraging a month of fine weather at the sea-coast, I was thrown into the company of a fascinating creature; two men took me by the limbs and hurled me through the window at the feet of a beautiful girl. It was love at first sight, but under her gaze I shrank into myself. I did this by withdrawing my head into my shirt through the collar. When I came out again she was gone.[2]

Meantime, back at Heathcliff's. I tried to stroke the

[2] What has this got to do with Wuthering Heights? *Ed.*

mother of six puppies; she sneaked wolfishly to the back of my leg, which she tried to take off.

'You'd better leave that dog alone,' growled Heathcliff, giving the dog a punch with his foot on which he kept a boxing-glove. The dog was now taking the front off my leg. 'She's not accustomed to being spoiled.' Heathcliff strode to a side door. He shouted, 'MacGonigle?' No one of that name lived here, so he strode to the other side and shouted, 'Napoleon? Julius Caesar? Robin Hood?' but no one answered till he called 'Joseph'.

Joseph mumbled indistinctly in the depths of the cellar, 'Indistinctly in the depths of the cellar,' he mumbled. Heathcliff dived down to him, leaving me with the dog affixed to my leg, she was joined by three snarling alsatians. Not wanting to arouse them further I tried to placate them: I indulged in winking, making faces, crossing my eyes, pulling my ears out, whereupon all four attacked my body from head to foot, dragging me around the room. As though inspired I called out 'Help'. I was saved by the cook.

She soothed the dogs with an RSPCA rolling-pin. Heathcliff came up, 'What the devil is that bundle of rags doing in the corner?'

'What the devil indeed!' I said. 'That's me!'

'Those dogs do right to be vigilant. Take a glass of wine?'

'Where to?' I said.

'What would you like?'

'A blood transfusion.'

He raised his glass. 'Your health, sir.'

'At the moment I haven't got any,' I said.

'Come, come,' he said. 'Take a little wine, guests are exceedingly rare in this house. The dogs eat 'em, you see. You're one of the lucky ones.'

Being a lucky one, I stood up and using safety-pins pulled my clothes together, keeping my eyes on the dogs. I bade him goodnight and walked backwards out of the room, first mistakenly backing into a meat-safe, where a ham fell on me rendering me unconscious.

When I regained consciousness, my host had kindly laid me in the snow at the front door. I found him fascinating, I was encouraged to volunteer another visit on the morrow. 'Oh, Christ,' he was heard to say.

Chapter II

NEXT DAY I was in two minds, whether to stay by my fire or go to Wuthering Heights so I tossed up for it: I came down heavily on my back. I told my housekeeper, a matronly lady taken as a fixture along with the house (she was screwed to the floor), that I was going out. Stepping into the study I saw a servant girl on her knees, polishing the floor. The temptation was great, but, by dousing my parts in cold water, the temptation passed. I put on my hat, and after a ten-mile walk arrived at Heathcliff's, two miles away. Heavy snow was falling. Unable to remove the chain on the gate, I jumped over, landing face down on the other side: by stuffing snow down my back, I stopped the nose bleed. I knocked and knocked the front door till my knuckles were raw, and the dogs howled: because of their threat, I was wearing eight pairs of trousers, riding-boots and a cricketer's box.

'Wretched inmates!' I ejaculated mentally. 'I *will* get in!' I ejaculated loudly. I grasped the latch and shook it vehemently: vehemently it came off. A young man appeared and beckoned me to follow him.

'This way, you silly sod,' he ejaculated. We went through a coal-shed, a pigeon-cote where I was covered in it. We arrived in a warm cheerful apartment, there was a huge fire compounded of coal, peat and wood. I threw on a spare piece of paper to add to the blaze. I observed the lady of the house was there. I bowed low, thinking she would bid me to take a seat, she didn't so I bowed lower, as low as my cricketer's box allowed before penetrating my scrotum. Looking at me she gracefully spat on the fire.

'Sit down,' said the young man gruffly, then he spat on the fire almost putting it out. As I sat, the mother dog growled at me.

'A beautiful animal,' I said. I was ready to wink at her in case she attacked me. 'Rough weather,' I said to the lady.

'Rough,' she said. 'It's fucking terrible.'

Seeing some cats on a cushion I said, 'Are your favourite cats among these?'

'Are you daft?' she said, then I realized they were not cats but dead rabbits. There it was, I couldn't tell a dead rabbit from a cat.

I hemmed and drew closer to the hearth. As I did the mother dog snarled at me, and I had to start winking and pulling faces as fast as I could.

As the lady stood near the fire for another gob at it, I could see how young and beautiful she was. For some reason I said, 'Will you marry me?' and she said, 'No, I'm already married.'

'Would you like to try it for a second time with me, just from the waist down?'

This time she spat in my eye. Somehow it killed my romantic illusion.

Meanwhile, the young man had slung on to his person a shabby upper garment, he then erected himself before the blaze. Obviously it was erecting time at Wuthering

Heights! He looked down on me from the corner of his eyes, as though for all the world there was some mortal unavenged feud between us. I asked him, 'Is there some unavenged feud between us?' The entrance of Heathcliff stopped me just as I was about to sing Psalm 39. 'You see, sir, I have come according to my promise of yesterday!' I exclaimed.

'Oh, Christ,' muttered Heathcliff.

Cheerfully I said, 'I fear I shall be weather-bound for half an hour if you can afford me shelter during that space.'

'Afford you shelter?' he said. '*Look*, I can't even afford the bloody rates.'

During this exchange I noticed he was snowing heavily, in some places it was knee high and this was indoors. 'Perhaps,' I said, 'as a guide to see me home, you could lend me one of your lads and he can stay at the Grange till morning.'

'No, I bloody can't,' he said. 'How do I know you are not a paedophile?'

'I give up,' I said. 'How do you know?'

He looked at me and called out an area of the female anatomy. He shook his head releasing flakes of snow but on inspection I realized it was dandruff, which he had a fine head of.

'Umph,' he said. I knew not what 'umph' meant, but I congratulated him in his choice of the word. He called me by the female part again. 'Now, sir,' said Heathcliff. 'Bring forward your chair.' We all sat around the dinner table, as we ate in grim silence – between each mouthful they all looked up to glower at me. I thought, if I had caused the cloud, it was my duty to dispel it.

'Rough weather,' I said. 'Mr Heathcliff, I'll venture to say how wonderful it must be in your home sur-

rounded by your family.' I paused as the lady gobbed
over the table into the fireplace. '. . . by your family and
with your amiable lady as the –.'

'My amiable lady!' he interrupted, a diabolical sneer
spread over his face and ran down his back to his nethers.
'Where is she – my amiable lady?'

'Mrs Heathcliff is my daughter-in-law,' said Heathcliff. Putting a boxing-glove on his foot he punched
the dog again, as he spoke he looked at Mrs Heathcliff
he gave her a peculiar look; raising and lowering his
eyebrows at great speed, at the same time activating
all the perverse muscles in his face at the same time
standing on one leg and whistling the National
Anthem.

'Ah, certainly – I see now; you are the favoured
possessor of the beneficent fairy,'[1] remarked my
neighbour.

This was worse than before. The youth grew crimson:
most of it going into his ears, which swelled to thrice
their size. I feared an attack, but he seemed to collect
himself, and he went around collecting the pieces. He
muttered a brutal curse on my behalf, again it was
female anatomy.

'Sir,' said Heathcliff, 'we neither of us have the
privilege of owning your good fairy.'[2]

'Her mate is dead.[3] I said she was my daughter-in-law,
therefore, she must have married my son,' said
Heathcliff.

'Then this young man with the red ears is . . .?'

'Not my son, assuredly!'

---

[1] Who she is no one knows.
[2] Who she is no one knows.
[3] Baffling. *Ed*.

Heathcliff smiled, as if it were rather too bold a jest to attribute the paternity of that oaf to him. The oaf spoke.

'Der – my name is – der – Hareton Earnshaw, and I'll – der - counsel you to respect it!'

He grabbed me by the lapels, ripping them off.

'I've shown no disrespect,' was my reply, laughing internally at the way he announced himself.

'Stop laughing at me internally,' he growled, ripping the sleeves off my jacket.

Heathcliff gave the dog a punch. 'It's kick boxing, it comes from Siam!' he said.

The meal being over (most of it over the floor), I approached a window to examine the weather.

It was suffocating with snow.

'I don't think it's possible to get home now without a guide,' I could not help exclaiming.

'Hareton, put the sheep into the barn, they'll die outdoors,' said Heathcliff.

'How must I do?' I continued with rising irritation. It had risen slowly from my feet to my knees. It was the worst rising since the Indian Mutiny. There was no reply to my question.

I saw Joseph bring in a pail of porridge for the kick box dogs and throw them in it, then in cracked tones he said, 'Aw woonder hagh yah can porridge faishion tuh stand thear i' idleness wi wan porridge when all 'ems goan aght grollik narg.'

I thought saying 'pardon?' was the best I could do.

'Is thart best u can do?' he said.

'You old reprobate,' said Mrs Heathcliff. 'Be off or I'll hurt you seriously. I'll have you modelled in clay, then snip important things off your body.' The little witch put a mock malignity into her beautiful eyes, and Joseph, trembling with hirrer, hurrer, and horror, stricken again with a laundry problem and porridge, hurried out praying for the most important things on his body.

'Mrs Heathcliff,' I said. 'I'm sure you cannot help being kind-hearted. Could you point out some land-marks to help me get home?'

'There's one,' she said, and pointed to the front door.

'I hope this will be a lesson to you to make rash bloody journeys in weather like this,' cried Heathcliff's stern voice from the kitchen. Having a voice in his stern seemed not to bother him. 'As to staying here, you'll have to sleep with Joseph, our resident homosexual.' With this insult, my patience ran out and down the road. I uttered an expression of disgust, 'Old Arab bum!' and pushed past him into the yard, colliding with a young wretch, who was training to be heavyweight champion of the world.

'I'll go with 'ee as far as the park,' he said.

'You'll go with him to hell,' exclaimed his master.

'I don't know that way, zur,' snivelled the lad rolling himself into a foetal position in the snow. In that position Heathcliff rolled him out the front gate and down the hill, where he finished up as a snowball and heavyweight champion of the world.

'I hope that lad's ghost haunts 'ee,' said Mrs Heathcliff.

In the shed by a lantern Joseph sat within earshot, so Heathcliff shot it, he was milking a cow.

I snatched the lantern, promising to return it on the morrow. Leaving him milking in Braille, I rushed to the nearest postern, then realized I hadn't snatched a lantern but a bucket of milk.

It would have to do.

On opening the little door, two hairy monsters flew

at my throat, bearing me down and extinguishing the milk, while a mingled laughter came from Heathcliff and Hareton, ha-mingle-ha. I was forced to lie still till their malignant selves pleased to deliver me. I ordered the miscreants to let me up.

Then winking at speed, I made several incoherent threats of retaliation, the vehemence of my agitation brought on a copious nose bleed. I managed to stem the flow by sticking a carrot up each nostril, knowing they contained Vitamin C. Heathcliff roared with insane laughter. To calm my rage I put on my hat, and to let him know I meant business, I put it on at a jaunty angle. To come and see what the uproar was Zillah, a stout housewife came in.

'Well, Mr Earnshaw,' she said, 'Are we going to murder folk on our own door-step? Look at t'poor lad, he's blocked up with carrots,' she said, pulling the dogs off my neck. 'Wisht, wisht, I'll cure that nose bleed.'

With these words she suddenly poured down my neck a bucket of icy washing-up water containing knives, forks and spoons which lodged in my trousers impacting heavily with my reproductive organs. As I clutched that area to remove the cutlery, Heathcliff and Hareton howled with laughter. I was dizzy and faint, I reeled backwards, I reeled forwards, then upright; as I revived, Zillah ushered me to a bedroom, saying, 'Usha, usha!'

'All fall down,' I said.

Chapter III

HEADING THE WAY upstairs Zillah told me not to make a noise. Her master had an odd notion about the chamber she would put me in. I asked the reason. She did not know, there had been many 'queer goings-on'. My God they're *all* homosexual, I thought. Zillah opened a door.

'Is this my chamber for the night?' I said.

'No,' she smiled. 'That's under the bed. If you use it, don't put it back as the steam rusts the springs,' she said.

Alone, I fastened my door. I blocked the keyhole in case someone used it for a base purpose. By my bed I placed my candle on a window-ledge. It was covered with scratched writings and names, *Catherine Earnshaw*, then *Catherine Heathcliff*, and again *Catherine Linton*. What a goer! Here was evidence she had had it away with three different men, or had it away once and changed her name twice.

In vapid listlessness I leant my head against the window but so heavy with ice and frost was it, my head stuck to it. Wrenching my head away, part of the pane stuck to it, I managed to wrench it off, but my hair stuck to it, leaving me with a bald patch, which I disguised with some soot from the chimney. I tried to sleep but couldn't, then I remembered I was standing up.

That discovered, I lay down and closed my eyes. I had
not been asleep five minutes when a glare of white
letters started from the dark, the Bradford and Bingley,
the air swarmed with Catherines. I tried to rouse myself,
I discovered my candle resting on old books. I snuffed it
out and started to read:[1] 'Catherine Earnshaw, her book',
and a date some quarter of a century back, it took the
form of a regular diary.

'An awful Sunday!' it commenced. 'I wish my father
were back again. Hindley is a detestable substitute – his
conduct to Heathcliff is atrocious – H. and I are going to
rebel!'

I read a while then fell into a deep sleep. I was awakened
by an acorn branch tapping on the window, something I
always wanted. I reached through the broken pane to
snap it off, instead of which my hand closed on the
fingers of a little ice-cold hand, a nightmare of horrors
came over me and I said, 'Ahgggh!' I had to clench the
cheeks of my bum to stop an emittance of solids. I tried
to withdraw my hand but the hand clung to it.

'Let me in,' sobbed a voice.

'Who are you?' sobbed my voice.

'Catherine Linton, I've come home.'

I let go another 'Ahgggh!'

'I'd lost my way on the moor.'

'You wouldn't like it in here,' I said. 'They're all
bloody barmy.'

As I ahggghed, I discerned a child's face looking in.
'Let me in,' she wailed.

'Ahggh!' Now I was clenching the cheeks of my

---

[1] He's snuffed the candle out, now he's going to read? *Ed.*

bottom to their maximum. I hit the little hand with my boot and it withdrew taking my boot with it. Never mind, I still had one left. 'Begone,' I cried, 'before the sphincter gives way!'

'Twenty years,' mourned the voice, 'I've been a waif for twenty years.'

'Happy Birthday,' I sang.

She was trying to get in! I yelled aloud in a frenzy of fright. Footsteps approached.

'Has anyone yelled in a frenzy of fright?' Heathcliff appeared holding a candle. 'Is anyone here?' he said.

'You are,' I said.

'So I am,' he said, grinding his teeth. I was still in the dark portion of the room. 'Are you a chimneysweep?' he asked.

'No, it is only your guest, sir.'

'I've never had a chimneysweep as a guest before,' he said, crushing his nails into his palms, where they got stuck. I had to use a screwdriver to release them. He continued to grind his teeth to subdue a maxillary convulsion.

I told him, 'Mr Heathcliff, you can cure maxillary convulsions by taking Dr Clott's Liquid Gum Nourisher.'

He pretended not to hear by putting his fingers in his ears and saying, 'What?' But the maxillary convulsions had a result, when next he spoke several teeth shot out.

'Who showed you to this room?'

'It was your servant, Zillah,' I replied, flinging myself to the floor and rapidly resuming my clothing! 'I suppose', I said, 'she wanted proof that the room was haunted at my expense. Well, it came to a pound. Can I have it in cash?' I asked. I told him the moor was swarming with ghosts and goblins and the words of

Bradford and Bingley. 'No one will thank you for a dose in such a den.'

'No one has ever caught a dose in this den,' he said. 'Look, lie down and finish your night, but for Heaven's sake don't give any more yells in a frenzy of fright.'

'But if the little fiend had got in the window, she would have strangled me,' I said. I grabbed my throat and hung my tongue out to demonstrate.

I then recalled the association of Heathcliff and Catherine's name in the book and I said so.

'Zounds,' he said. 'How *dare* you talk like this under my roof!'

'I can say it again in the garden if you like,' I said. He struck his forehead the very moment a fly had landed flattening it. He fell back on my bed in the shadows.

'Mr Lockwood,' he said, getting off the bed and putting one foot in the po, 'Mr Lockwood, you may go into my room, you'll only be in the way here, and your yells in a frenzy of fright have sent sleep to the devil for me. Here, take this candle and bowl of porridge and wander where you please. Try Denmark.' He was breathing very heavily, you could hear it whistling and going clickity-click 'all the fours' down his nose.

I quit the chamber, *je suis sorti de la chambre*, but I got lost in the narrow lobbies, and I seemed to arrive back where I started, outside my room, and himmel! I saw Heathcliff, kneeling and sobbing through the broken window.

'Come in!' he sobbed. 'Oh, Cathy, my heart's darling, come and bring the boot with you.'

She who had spoken gave no sign of being, but the snow and wind swirled blowing out my candle.

I groped my way downstairs. It was the first good grope I'd had for years. I arrived in the back kitchen

with a fire from which I relit my candle. My foot
without the boot was freezing. I took off my vest and
covered it with that then tying it up with bits of string.
From there I could still hear the distant drooling of
Heathcliff over Cathy interrupted by violent clicks of his
nose.

There were two benches by the fire, one of which I
stretched on. When I lay down I was 5 feet 9 inches,
then stretched 6 feet. On the other bench was a cat
called Grimalkin. I fell into a deep sleep and awoke on
the floor, facing the fire with my trousers smouldering,
which I beat out, leaving two holes in the knees. Joseph
now on the second bench was sitting on the cat, smoking
a pipe 'Addum a t'nice sleepons oo?' he said. '*Je ne parle
pas français*,' I told him. A wisp of smoke escaped from
his pipe, he inserted a fresh wisp.

There entered Hareton Earnshaw performing his ori-
sons, such as 'Beyond the blue orison lies a beautiful
day,'[2] then taking the cat, Grimalkin by the tail he
swung it round and round his head. 'They did say there
was not room to swing a cat in here, that's proved them
wrong.'

He bade me follow him, leaving behind Grimalkin
with a tail now five feet long.

I was ushered into a room by Earnshaw by putting
the handle of a shovel in the small of my back and
shoving. Here all the females were astir. Zillah was astir
blowing the fire with a colossal bellows. There was
Mrs Heathcliff astir reading a book by the light of the
blaze.

Heathcliff was shouting at her. 'You will pay me for
the plague of having you eternally in my sight.'

[2] Thought by some to be a brilliant pun. *Ed*.

A look of beatitude came over that beautiful face. 'Why don't you piss off,' she said.

Heathcliff raised his left leg. 'Look out, he's going to do a butler's revenge,' she said, and sprang to a safer distance. I made to leave.

'Wait,' said Heathcliff, so saying, he grabbed a dog by the tail and swung it round his head. 'They do say there's no room to swing a cat in here, well, that proves them wrong.' I waited no further. I fled the house for home.

The distance from Wuthering Heights to the Grange is but two miles. Somehow I managed to do it in ten again. Several times coming here I had sunk up to my neck in snow and Heathcliff's dogs had urinated on my head. As I entered my home, a crowd rushed to welcome me. I don't know who they were, some say they were from a film agency. They had completely given me up and had sold most of my clothes. I dragged myself upstairs, whence after putting on dry clothes and a fresh boot I paced to and fro' for forty to fifty minutes to restore the animal heat. No matter how fast I walked I ended up in the same room.

Chapter IV

ADJOURNED TO my study weak as a kitten to enjoy a cheerful fire. Mrs Dean brought in my supper, as I ate, we talked.

'You have been here a considerable time, did you not say?'

'No, I did not say,' she said. 'I haven't said anything,' she said. By putting an arm lock on her she admitted to having worked here eighteen years.

'I came when the mistress was married to wait on her. After she died, I didn't see the point of waiting any longer. The master kept me on for groping duties. By the way, you look as weak as a kitten.'

'Indeed.'

There ensued a pause. I took advantage of this by doing some knees bend. She was not a gossip, I feared, unless about her own affairs (among which was a Chinaman). I had no interest. I asked her why Heathcliff had let Thrushcross Grange.

'Had let it, what?' she said.

'Rented it,' I ejaculated.

'He let it for money,' she said.

'He had a son?'

'Yes.'

'Is he dead?'

'I think so, they buried him.'

'And Mrs Heathcliff is his widow?'[1]

'Yes, she is my late master's daughter. Catherine Linton was her maiden name.'

'What? Catherine Linton!!!' I ejaculated in a shower of spittle that showered Mrs Dean. She had to sponge her glasses before she could see again. While she did, I did some press-ups to keep me fit. 'Who is Hareton Earnshaw?' I said.

'That bastard is the late Mrs Linton's nephew.'

'Is that who the bastard is?' I inquired.

'Yes, he is the last of the Earnshaws. Isn't that good?' she said, clapping her hands together. 'When you were a guest at Wuthering Heights, how was Cathy?'

'Mrs Heathcliff? She looked very well, handsome, not very happy and a pain in the arse. She likes reading books by the fireside, she's all scorched down one side.'

'What about her master, Heathcliff? He's so mean, if he were a ghost he'd be too mean to give you a fright,' she said.

'He must have had some ups and down in his life,' I said.

'Yes,' she agreed. 'He used to be a lift attendant.'

Excited by this information, I asked for more. 'Very well,' she said, folding her arms and putting them on her knitting basket. 'I used to be at Wuthering Heights.'

'So, you used to be at Wuthering Heights.'

'I used to play with the children, and I used to run errands too,' she said.

'So,' I said, 'you used to run errands too?'

'Yes, they never let me walk.'

'So, they never let you walk,' I said.

---

[1] Even I am baffled. *Ed.*

'Look!' she said, shaking me by the throat. 'For Christ's sake, will you stop interrupting.' For a while I lay on the floor doing sit-ups.

'One fine summer morning', she continued, 'Mr Earnshaw, the old master, came down dressed for a journey. He wore a tram driver's uniform. "You going by tram?" we said. "No," he said, "I'm going by uniform." He turned to Hindley and Cathy. "Now, I'm going to Liverpool. What shall I bring you?" Hindley named a fiddle, he named it Dick. Cathy chose a whip, for strict discipline. The lunatic set off to walk sixty miles there, and sixty back. We waved him goodbye, some waved him goodbye for ever. He was gone three days, then one midnight he returned. He threw himself at a chair and missed.

'He opened his great coat, holding a bundle in his arms. We crowded round to see a dark, ragged black-haired child. "Aye up!" said Mrs Earnshaw. "Aye," said Mr Earnshaw. The child was talking in a language we could not understand. "It's Pakistani." The master tried to explain. The children refused to have the child in bed with them or even in the room. They called him Heathcliff. Bit by bit, they got used to him. First a bit of his leg, a bit of his arm, bit of his teeth and so on, he got on very well with Cathy, and said one day they would open up a corner shop in Leeds. To Cathy it was magic!

'Hindley hated him and frequently rendered the boy senseless with an iron bar. Then Heathcliff went ill with measle, just one measle. I stayed by his bed all night, every hour giving him spoonfuls of curry. Despite this, he recovered. By now we all doted on him, he was covered with dote marks. Hindley hated him, he had seen him naked in the bath, and was jealous of his porportions.

'Then Mrs Earnshaw died, worn out with making curry for Heathcliff. Cathy and her brother love practical jokes like practising setting fire to me. Mr Earnshaw bought a couple of horses, a lover of horse flesh, he looked forward to eating one. Heathcliff took one and Hindley the other. But Heathcliff's horse went lame in the teeth that kept falling out. "You must exchange the horses," said Heathcliff. Hindley gave Heathcliff his horse. "You better hurry up and ride it, because Mr Earnshaw is having it for dinner." '

Chapter V

*I*N THE COURSE of time Mr Earnshaw started to fail. Only that morning he had failed to come down with his trousers on, his strength suddenly left him: it left by the back door. People in the street would say, "Look, there goes Mr Earnshaw's strength." Mr Earnshaw said he was worried about the welfare of Heathcliff after he died. I said after he died Heathcliff wouldn't need any welfare. "No, no, I mean after *my* death," said Mr Earnshaw. There was talk of sending Heathcliff to school, but no school would take him. Heathcliff was delighted. No, his was a free, wild life on the moors making chapattis and tandoori on the wood fire.

'Cathy was much too fond of Heathcliff. The greatest punishment would be for her to be kept separate from Heathcliff. When they were they had to be prised apart with a crowbar.

'Now, Mr Earnshaw did not understand jokes. Cathy said, "I say, I say, I say, what's a Jewish dilemma?" Earnshaw didn't know. "It's pork chops at half price,"[1] she said. By now overwhelmed by Cathy's jokes, Heath-

[1] Early stages of Nazism. *Ed.*

cliff was completely under her spell. He would do her
bidding in anything. After behaving badly all day, she
would come innocent fondling to make it up at night.
"Stop that innocent fondling, and get your clothes on,"
said old Earnshaw. "Go, say thy prayers to the Lord,
now piss off." So happily she pissed off.

'But not long after, Mr Earnshaw too pissed off; he
died quietly, so quietly no one heard him go. "I can't
hear anything," said Cathy. "That must be him dying."
I was sitting by the hearth knitting, Joseph was reading
the Bible, Miss Cathy had her head in her father's lap,
Heathcliff was lying on the floor with his head in her lap
– they looked like contortionists. Cathy was in the
middle of telling Mr Earnshaw a joke when suddenly
she realized Mr Earnshaw had snuffed it. She screamed
out, "Oh, he's dead, Heathcliff! He's dead. Quick, the
policy." She burst into tears. "He'll never eat horse meat
again!" she said. "He's never done this before," said
Heathcliff. Joseph told me to run for the doctor. I
couldn't see what use either would be. The doctor
arrived, he examined Mr Earnshaw. "This man is dead,"
he said. "That will be two guineas."'

Chapter VI

MR HINDLEY came home for the funeral. He had brought his wife so she could enjoy it too.

'Now it was Young Earnshaw who was the new master – since a boy he had changed. He had grown sparer, it was growing everywhere, in fact he was covered in it, and he dressed differently with his trousers back to front, against high tide. He told me that we must quarter ourselves in the back kitchen. Mr Hindley took over the rest of the house. He became tyrannical, he only allowed Heathcliff to work outdoors, he refused him his curry, forcing him to eat sausage and chips. It broke his heart. Many times Joseph would thrash Heathcliff to warm himself up, and Cathy would be denied her dinner. Heathcliff and Cathy would run away in the mornings to the moors returning late at night, shagged out. Many a time I cried to myself to watch them daily becoming more reckless every day. Sometimes she'd go without knickers. As to the new mistress Mrs Earnshaw, she was not a well woman, mounting the stairs made her breathless and she had to stop, it took her three days to get to the first floor. She was very thin, causing a constant falling off of her clothes. I tell you, Mr Lockwood, it was not a happy home.

'One Sunday evening as Cathy and the Pakistani

practised Sumo wrestling they were banished from the
sitting room for grunting. When I went to call them for
supper, they had gone. We searched everywhere, but
they were not there, so they must be somewhere else.
"Sod them," said Mr Hindley, and bolted the doors for
the night. I sat on my bed listening. I heard footsteps
approaching. I threw a shawl over my head and ran into
the wall. At the door was Heathcliff. It gave me a start.

'Having started, I said, "Where's Cathy?" "Let me
get my wet clothes off," he said. I bade him beware of
rousing the master, and while he undressed I caught
sight of his twelve inches, and had to stifle a cry of
delight. "We ran from here to Thrushcross Grange,"
said Heathcliff. "Cathy won because she was barefoot."
He continued, "We looked through the windows of the
Grange, the Linton children were there, Isabella lay
screaming at one end of the room, Edgar stood at the
other end crying, in the middle lay a dog yelping which
the children had nearly pulled in two, it lay there now
seven feet long. Then they saw us. "Run, Heathcliff,
run," Cathy whispered. "They have let the bulldog
loose, my leg is half way down its throat." Heathcliff
vociferated curses enough to annihilate any fiend in
Christendom, the dog seemed not to understand – perhaps he was deaf – so he got a rock, dropped it on his
head, then rammed it down his throat.

'A servant came running "Keep fast, Skulker, keep
fast." But when he saw Skulker he said, "Oh fuck." He
carried Cathy into the home while Heathcliff carried
Skulker. "What goes on?" halloed Mr Linton. "Skulker
has caught a little girl and this lad . . ." Mrs Linton came
forward. She looked at Heathcliff. "Be careful you don't
catch tandoori off him, they've all got it." They took
Cathy in to look after her leg, and they told Heathcliff
to bugger off.'

Chapter VII

" FEAR YOU have not heard the last of this," I said. Cathy stayed at Thrushcross Grange for five weeks, by which time her leg was better and Skulker was dead. She rode back on a handsome black horse. "Why, Cathy, you and your horse look quite beautiful," said Hindley as he patted them both. Indeed the stay at the Lintons had transformed her from a waif to a lady in fine clothes.

'"Nelly," said Hindley. "Help Cathy with her clothes."

'"Stay, dear," I said. "Let me untie your hat."

'"That's my head," said Cathy.

'"Then let me untie your head," I said. Then Cathy came down to the kitchen and kissed me. I was flour-making the Christmas cake. She hugged me and the Christmas cake came off on her. Then she looked round for Heathcliff.

'"Is Heathcliff not here?" she asked, pulling off her gloves, displaying wonderfully white fingers caused by doing nothing and staying indoors!

'"Heathcliff, come forward," cried Hindley. "If you can't come forward, come sideways!" Catching a glimpse of the Pakistani, Cathy flew to embrace him, and the Christmas cake came off on him. She bestowed

several or eight kisses on him, but, overwhelmed by the
smell of curry, she drew back, and laughed. "Why, how
black you are and grim."

'"Shake hands, Heathcliff," said Mr Earnshaw. Heathcliff shook his hands.

'"Now, what?" he said.

'"I didn't mean to laugh at you," said Cathy. "It's
only that you're so dirty."

'"I'll be as dirty as I please," he said, stuffing his hand
down his trousers and scratching his balls. "Yes, I'll be a
dirty bugger," he cried, throwing himself head foremost
out of the room, and landing on it outside.'

'After all this, I put my cakes in the oven for Christmas. I prepared to sit down and amuse myself by
singing carols all alone for which the doctor had given
me tablets to take until I was better. I remember how
old Mr Earnshaw would slip threepence into my hand as
a Christmas box, the mean bastard. One morning Heathcliff came to me,

'"Nelly, make me decent, make me clean."

'So I started on him with sandpaper and linseed oil
and, Mr Lockwood, he looked splendid! I talked to him,
"Who knows but your father was the Emperor of
China, and your mother an Indian queen, and you were
kidnapped by wicked sailors."

'"You've got it wrong. My father was a dustman in
Bombay," said Heathcliff, "All I want is for Cathy and
me to get a corner shop in Leeds."

'Outside, the Lintons and the Earnshaws were arriv-
ing back from church.

'"Bloody good sermon," said Mr Linton. Hindley
entered the room. On seeing Heathcliff all clean he said,
"*Quelle horreur.*" For reason of snobbishment he spoke
in French. "Keep that *garçon* out of this *chambre.*"

'Master Linton entered. Seeing Heathcliff he said, "It's the curry *garçon*." Heathcliff seized a tureen of porridge and threw it in the boy's face. Cathy rushed in.

'"Heathcliff," she shrieked. "What have you done?"

'"I've just done him," he said.

'Seeing Master Linton covered in porridge, Cathy said, "You're wearing our breakfast."

'Heathcliff took Cathy by the hand. "Come, let us go and buy a corner shop."

'Hindley grabbed Heathcliff and flung him upstairs. "*A tout à l'heure*," he shouted after him.

'"Fuck *vous*," came the reply.

'Poor Master Linton was crying. "Don't cry," said Cathy. "It will ruin the porridge."

'After lunch, we were entertained by the Gimmerton band. Mrs Earnshaw loved the music and danced round the fire holding a chair; everyone agreed she looked like an idiot. Cathy said that music sounded better from upstairs, where she fled. I followed her: she went to the garret where Heathcliff was confined, she looked through the keyhole and could see Heathcliff on his prayer mat worshipping towards Mecca. She then clambered over the roof and had got into his room through the skylight.[1] Downstairs Mrs Earnshaw was now dancing with a table and later the grandfather clock; it was good clean Victorian fun, which made the heart joyous. Alas! the clock fell on her at exactly one-thirty p.m. In Heathcliff's garret, Cathy asked him why he was bobbing up and down. "I am praying to Allah."

'"Won't he keep still? Oh," said Cathy, "where is he?"

'"He's dead," said Heathcliff.

[1] There was no need because the door was open. *Ed.*

'Cathy looked puzzled, she laid a hand on his shoulder. "Are you all right? Shouldn't you see a doctor?"

'I let the couple converse uninterrupted, then I told them the coast was clear, in case they wanted to go there, and they both came down into the kitchen. He had not eaten since yesterday's vindaloo. I set him on a stool by the fire, I offered him a quantity of good things, a carriage clock, a travelling case, camera, a set of monogrammed golf clubs, a cuddly toy. "No, I'm not hungry," he said. "All I want is to pay Hindley back, he has beaten me black and blue."

'I had to point out the black was there in the first place. But, Mr Lockwood, I'm annoyed how I should dream of chattering on at such a rate (one pound an hour) and your gruel cold, and you nodding for bed, and you weak as a kitten. The clock is on the stroke of eleven, sir.'

'Nevertheless, Mrs Dean, resume your chair; because tomorrow I intend lengthening the night till afternoon. I prognosticate for myself an obstinate cold at least.'

What a crashing bore this man is, thought Mrs Dean.

'Very well, Mr Lockwood, will you allow me to leap over some three years?'

'No, no,' said the crashing bore. 'I'll allow nothing of the sort. Are you acquainted with the mood of mind in which, if you were seated alone, and the cat is licking its kitten –' Please, God, stop him, prayed Mrs Dean. '. . . on the rug before you, you would watch an operation so intently that puss's neglect of one ear would put you seriously out of temper.'

'I'm sorry, Mr Lockwood, I don't understand a word you're saying. Can I continue?'

Lockwood nodded, then winced with a pain in his neck which he was.

'It was the summer of 1778 . . . .' continued Mrs Dean.

Chapter VIII

ON A FINE June day, the last Earnshaw was born. Alas! the mother was with consumption and, sure enough, she snuffed it, and Mr Earnshaw raced to Liverpool to cash in the policy. The child called Hareton fell wholly into my hands, which he often filled. With the policy money Mr Earnshaw turned to drink: he started with lemonade, but that soon lost its hold over him, and he turned to that fiend from hell, whisky. Insane on alcohol he would run on to the road and expose himself to passing carriages, but it still couldn't match Heathcliff's. The master's bad ways set a pretty bad example for Cathy and Heathcliff; his treatment of the latter was terrible. He made the latter work all hours, he denied the latter proper meals, he also stopped the latter's pay. It made the former very sad, people would say, "What's the matter former?" But Cathy still had great attraction for the latter. I could not tell what an infernal home we had. Every night Hindley would stagger in drunk with his flies open and sick down the front; he became famous in the district for his flashing. The curate stopped calling. The gas man came and read the meter and asked who the author was.

'Occasionally Edgar Linton called to see Miss Cathy.

At fifteen she was queen of the countryside, she had no peer, a terrible anatomical shortcoming. One afternoon Hindley went out on a flashing expedition, so Heathcliff, on the strength of it, gave himself a holiday. Cathy and he were constant companions, he had ceased to express his fondness for her in words, instead he would do a series of somersaults ending up with a cry of "Hola" but he recoiled from her girlish caresses. As they caused great heat in the trousers and the smell of burning hairs, he took a jug of water and poured it down his trousers. When the steam had abated, Heathcliff announced he would not work that day. "But", said Cathy, "Joseph will tell Hindley."

'"Joseph is shovelling shit at the manure tip, he'll never know," so saying Heathcliff squatted down by the fire and started to make chapattis and chant a raga.

'"Hindley doesn't like wily oriental music," said Cathy.

'"It's a big hit in Calcutta," said Heathcliff.

'"I must tell you", said Cathy, "that Isabella and Edgar Linton . . " At the mention of them Heathcliff winced and let fall his chapatti. ". . . They talked of calling this afternoon."

'"I, too," said Heathcliff, "talked of calling this afternoon – I was going to call it Tuesday." It was a joke. It died there in that room with Cathy as a mourner. He was going to top it with, "Why did the chicken cross the road?", but there came the sound of horses' hooves and dung. Young Linton entered grinning and waggling his eyebrows. A well-meaning nerd. Heathcliff rolled up his chappatis and with a lewd gesture left.

'Miss Cathy was furious, she stamped her tiny foot on the floor, dislocating her toe. In pain she hopped round the room holding her foot. Eventually she came to rest where Master Linton passed the time of day with her.

'"Two-thirty and five seconds," he said.

'I was polishing the EPNS when Cathy said; "Nelly, leave the room!" I told her I couldn't because Mr Hindley had said I was never to leave her alone with male company.

'Cathy smiled. "Whatever for?" she said.

'"In case they fucked you, miss."

'She laughed. "Fuck me? I'm sure that's the last thing Master Linton would do, would you, Edgar?"

'"Oh, no," he said, "I wouldn't wait that long."

'Cathy threw back her head and shrieked with laughter.

'"Do you still see Heathcliff?" asked Master Linton.

'"Yes," said Cathy, "in the wind and the rain. He and I run across the moors until we're knackered, then in the wind and the rain we run back till we're knackered again."

'Master Linton said, "How often do you do this?"

'"Three days a week," said Cathy.

'"What do you get out of it?" asked Linton.

'"Bronchitis," said Cathy.

'Again she asked me to leave the room. I declined, she rushed up and pinched me with a long powerful pinch on my bottom.

'I jumped up and screamed, "You have no right to nip my nethers."

'She denied it, her ears going red with rage. "I never nipped you," she screamed.

'In a flash I raised my skirt, dropped my drawers and exposed the bruise on my nethers. Before anyone could stop her she got a walking-stick and gave my nethers a wallop.

'"I don't love you any more," I cried. I heard Master Linton mutter he had never seen such a "huge arse".'

Chapter IX

AT THIS STAGE Earnshaw came in raving drunk, he crashed in through the window, mistaking it for the door. There was glass everywhere, mostly in him; as he got to his feet he let go a monstrous fart. It scorched a hole in the back of his trousers. I retired into the kitchen with little Hareton to hide him. Earnshaw burst into the room, he grabbed me by the scuff of the arm.

'"I'm going to make you swallow a carving knife."

'I told him straight, "Mr Earnshaw, I don't like swallowing carving knives."

'"For Heaven's sake, why not?" He looked disappointed. "Something else, then, how about a soup ladle?" He offered me many things to swallow, a Broadwood 1818 piano, a mangle, but I just didn't fancy it. Finally, he settled for beans on toast. It was a near thing.

'He grabbed little Hareton, who was screaming and yelling,

'"Mr Hindley!" I appealed, as he took the child upstairs and hung him over the banisters. "He needs changing," I said.

'"Good, change him for a hall chair," he said and let go of the child.

'In a flash, in one bound, from nowhere appeared Heathcliff, who caught the child. "Oh goodness, gracious," he said. "*Von* second more and that child would have gone splat!"

'Earnshaw went white with fury, red with rage and purple with apoplexy, finally green with envy. "How dare you stop my child going splat," he raged and dribbled.

' "Did you vant him to die?" said Heathcliff.

' "No," said Earnshaw, "I just wanted him to go splat. Can't a decent man let his child go splat?"

'I took the baby from Heathcliff as half of it was over him. Earnshaw poured a measure of brandy. "No!" I cried, grabbing the glass and drank it all to stop his drunken ways. He drained the bottle, then went upstairs shouting that there would be some changes made.

'I was rocking Hareton on my knee, humming a song that went: "Ee I addio – we are the champions." Then horror! down the stairs flaunted Mr Earnshaw, wearing a blonde lady's wig, a tight-fitting scarlet velvet dress, off-the-shoulder, white frilly trouser drawers, silk stockings and mid-calf, button-up bootees.

' "Mr Earnshaw, that's your late wife's dress."

'He laughed as he applied powder and rouge to his face. "I said there'd be some changes made, this is one of them." He hummed the *Blue Danube* and danced around the room, then ran out in the night towards the Black Bull Inn.

'Where would it all end? Supposing he met a sailor, who would do what to who and how? I must say he did look lovely. I had resumed singing: "Ee I addio" when Cathy came in.

' "Where is Heathcliff?" she asked.

' "He's in the stable shovelling dung," I said.

'She looked up with her beautiful face and said,

"There must be other things than dung in life, Nelly?" I told her that Heathcliff's ambition was for she and him to open a corner shop in Leeds, till then he had to shovel dung.

'"Nelly, can you keep a secret?"

'Keep a secret, I thought, wait till I tell her about *Earnshaw*! I was still trying to get this little bastard Hareton to sleep.

'"Today," said Cathy, "Edgar Linton asked me to marry him. He went down on one knee, so heavily he could hardly carry on. He read the terms of the marriage contract, in the event of a split we'd go fifty fifty. I'll get the gas stove. As yet I have not said yea or nay. Tell me, Nelly, what ought it to be?"

'The baby let out a shriek. "Quiet, baby darling," I said, pouring the remains of the brandy down him. "Cathy," I said, "I can't tell you yea or nay, that's up to you."

'"Well," she said, "I love the ground under his feet and the air over his head." "That's all very well," I said. "But what about *him*?"

'Cathy stood up with a triumphant smile, so saying she pirouetted and fell back on the floor, lying there a while unconscious, her eyes slightly crossed. Eventually she came to and admitted to me that she had accepted Edgar's proposal of marriage. Then she lowered her voice to a deep baritone, she did it by crossing her legs and pressing hard with her right hand into her crotch. "It would have degraded me to marry Heathcliff, so he will never know how much I loved him and his curries. He's more myself than I am."

'So I asked her who she was. "What are souls made of, both our souls are the same," she said.

'"So you both have the same arsole?" I said.

'I suddenly became aware of Heathcliff's presence – just a whiff of garlic, ghee and dung. He had heard all Cathy had to say. He arose from his bench and went into the night; likewise he went against the wall.

'"For this relief, much thanks, Horatio,"[1] he said as he shook the drips off. I told Cathy that when Heathcliff hears of her forthcoming marriage, he will be a broken man.

'"With modern science," said Cathy, "he can be togethered again."

'"As soon as you marry the nerd, Heathcliff will lose a friend, love and the five-mile knackering runs on the moor," I said.

'"No," she said. "Nothing will consent forsaking Heathcliff. I have felt his and he has felt mine and no one can take that away from us. My love for Linton is like the foliage in the woods, but my love for Heathcliff is like Chicken Madras. Nelly, I am Heathcliff."

'"Oh," I said, "then who is *he*?"

'"Don't you see, Nelly," she said, "*he is me*."

'"I see, you are both each other," I said.

'She smiled and nodded.

'Joseph interrupted our conversation. He spoke his traditional rubbish, "Und hah, isn't that nowt porridge comed in frough the' field be thus time? What is e a baht porridge girt eedle seeght Heathcliff e?"

'I called softly for Heathcliff.

'Softly he didn't answer.

'Cathy jumped up in a fine fright. The finest fright I had ever seen.

'I whispered to her that Heathcliff had heard a good part of what she had said.

'"Wait till he hears the bad part," she said, tapping

---

[1] Reference to *Hamlet*. *Ed*.

her nose but nothing fell out. Catherine paced up and
down the kitchen floor, sometimes she'd pace down and
then up. "Where is he, where is he? What did I say,
Nelly? I've forgotten."

'"You have just said, 'where is he, where is he?'" I
said. I had administered the last of the brandy to little
Hareton who was now pissed and fast asleep.

'Meantime, Mr Earnshaw had come home via the
back stairs so Miss Cathy didn't see him in drag. He had
a wonderful time with a guardsman at the Black Bull
Inn. Cathy had gone running across the moor looking
for Heathcliff. A terrible storm broke out over Wuthering Heights and Cathy barefoot and beautiful ran across
the drenching moor calling Heathcliff's name. She
would pause on tiptoe, cup her dainty hand to her
sweet lips and call "Heathcliff!!!". A tree fell on her.
Unhurt but trapped to the ground she called, "Heathcliff, where the fuck are you?" By dawn she had managed to extricate herself from the tree, she arrived home
soaked, to be greeted by Hindley who had just removed
his make-up.

'"What ails you?" he said.

'"A tree ailed me," she said.

'I witnessed this as I had come down early to give the
baby his morning bottle of brandy.

'"But Cathy, you're soaking wet," said Hindley.

'"Yes, that's what rain does," she said steaming by the
fire.

'She called to me, "Nelly, shut the window, I'm
starving."

'So I shut the window to stop her starving.

'"Were you with Heathcliff last night?" asked
Hindley.

'"No, I was with a tree," sobbed Cathy. "If you turn

Heathcliff out of the doors," she sobbed, "I'll turn out with him." She sobbed into the fire putting it out.

'"She's ill," said Hindley taking her wrist; then taking her ankle he dragged her sobbing upstairs and put her in bed. Hindley lavished on her a torrent of abuse, then taking pity he sang a chorus of *Auld Lang Syne* in Swedish. I thought she was going mad. I begged Joseph to run for Dr Kenneth.

'"If Aw wor yah maister Awd just slam t'boards porridge I'their farses" he said

'"All right," I said. "No, get the bloody doctor."

'Dr Kenneth came. "This girl should be in bed," he said.

'"She is in bed," I said.

'"I'm glad you agree with my diagnosis," he said. "This girl is very ill, she has a fever." He bled her, and told me to let her live on whey and water-gruel and keep the windows locked in case of starvation, and that would be five pounds. In her delirium Cathy called out, "Ohh, ohh, Heathcliff twelve inches, oh oh, Linton only six." She was a difficult patient. Old Mrs Linton visited her, she insisted that we weren't treating her properly. She insisted on taking Cathy to Thrushcross Grange, for this deliverance we were grateful, but alas! Mrs Linton was to repent her kindness, she and her husband caught the fever and died within a few days of each other. Having killed them, Miss Cathy returned to us, saucier, passionate and haughtier than ever.

'Heathcliff had never been heard of since the night of the thunderstorm, when he fled leaving behind a packet of curry and a tube of pile ointment. "How he must have suffered without them," said Miss Cathy. From now on she treated me at a distance, sometimes over a mile. Joseph would speak his mind, sometimes he would speak his leg. Every day Cathy would search the moor for her beloved Heathcliff with the wind and the rain in her hair. She took with her his pile ointment in case they met.

'By now she knew Earnshaw was a transvestite. She had to hide all her clothes from him. "I don't want his wedding tackle going in my knickers," she said with a naughty smile.

'"Oh, you needn't have worried, Miss Cathy, he's had the operation, he is now Gladys Earnshaw. He's very popular, he's always being invited to balls though he himself hasn't got any," I said.'

Chapter X

EDGAR LINTON was the happiest nerd alive when he led Cathy to the altar at Gimmerton Chapel. While standing there they decided to get married. They honeymooned in a bedroom. You could hear the screams a mile away. Miss Cathy wanted me to leave Wuthering Heights and join her here. By now Hareton was five years old and a life member of Alcoholics Anonymous. I was teaching him the alphabet and he had mastered the letter A. It was lovely to hear him say, "Der Der A!" I told her we didn't want to part, but Catherine's tears were more powerful than ours, she cried at the rate of two gallons an hour, in the end we had to swim for it. I told her I would never leave Wuthering Heights, never, never. Then Cathy looking beautiful gave me a very precious gift that made me change my mind. It was called money. I said goodbye to Hareton. "Der Der A," he said. The new mistress of Wuthering Heights was lovely Gladys Earnshaw and his lover Able-Seaman "Shagger" Macgee with a wooden leg which he used for terrible perversions on OAPs.

'So life started for me at Thrushcross. I observed that Mr Edgar had a deep-rooted fear of ruffling Cathy's sense of humour like pretending to have fits. If he was

displeased with the servants, he would show it with a
frown. "Look out!" we'd say, "he's going to frown!"
and hide ourselves.

'Catherine went on being beautiful but she had seasons
of gloom and silence. She also had fits of rage, fits of
crying, fits of laughter, but at all times the wild wind
and rain blew through her hair on the wild moor. They
called the doctor again. He got into her bed and examined her.

'"What is the verdict, Doctor?"

'The doctor shook his head. "Your wife is barmy.
That'll be fifty pounds."

'"Fifty pounds!" said Linton. "You must think I'm
barmy as well."

'"Then that will be another fifty pounds," said the
doctor.

'It seemed that when Cathy and Edgar were together,
she was especially happy, likewise when she was together. I don't think the marriage was ever consum-
mated, I think they both did it on their own; he started
to wear glasses.

'One evening I sat on the back step, scratching some
of my areas where no human eye had ever set foot. I
heard a voice say, "Nelly, is that you?" It was a deep
dark voice. Something stirred in the porch, there was a
faint scent of curry, a man came forward, it was a dark
man, I remembered his eyes. Last time he had two, yes it
was Heathcliff!

'He spoke hastily, "Where is she, Nelly? Does the
wild wind from the moor still blow through her hair?
Go and say a person from Gimmertom YMCA wants
to see her."

'"How will she take it?" I said.

'"Well, usually in a haystack," he said. I was so surprised.

'"You really *are* Heathcliff, but altered," I said.

'"Yes, Nelly, altered. I now dress on my right side. Now, go tell Cathy I'm here!"

'I went up and told her. "A person from the Gimmerton YMCA wishes to see you, m'am," I said.

'"What does he want?' said Mrs Linton.

'"He wants to see you in a haystack," I said, giving her a meaningful look, of which she knew not the meaning. "I must warn you he now dresses on his right side."

'"Bring up the tea," she said, and tripped gaily from the room.

'She was singing happily as she pitched headlong down the stairs. Ignoring her scream, Mr Edgar inquired carelessly who the stranger was.

'"It was Heathcliff."

'"What?" said Edgar. "The curry addict?"

'"Shh, Mr Edgar, you must not hurt him because of his curry," I said. "She was heartbroken when he ran off to find his dream corner shop. When she sees him again the wind from the wild moor will blow through her hair again even though now she has scurf."

'Hiding the bottle of Bell's whisky, a bargain at £2, Mr Linton went to the window and peered down. He liked a good peer. "Don't stand there, bring him up."

'So Catherine flew upstairs, breathless and wild. "Oh Edgar," she panted, flinging her arms around his neck, bringing them both crashing to the ground. With a yowl a cat flew under them. "Oh Edgar, darling, Heathcliff's come back."

'"Why?" managed to croak Mr Linton, trying to rise with Cathy hanging on his neck. "Nelly," he called. "Get her off me, she's strangling me."

'Grabbing Cathy by the ankles, I pulled her off, alas! also her drawers.

' "Oh, Heathcliff," cried Cathy. "He's back."

' "Look," said her cuckolded husband. "He's a curry addict."

' "I know you don't like him," she said, pulling up her drawers, the wind on the moor still blowing through her hair. "Shall I ask him to come up now?"

' "Here?" said Edgar, "into the parlour!!!?"

' "Where else?" she asked.

' "How about Calcutta?" he said. He finally suggested the laundry.

' "No, no," said Cathy.

' "Lay the table in here, Nelly," said Edgar. I bade Heathcliff step up, and with Catherine trying to control herself I showed Heathcliff in. Cathy shot across the floor and, throwing her arms around him, showered him with passionate kisses.

'Mr Linton stood watching them, eventually he sat down to watch them. Finally rising, "Ahem Ahem," he said, tapping Heathcliff on the shoulder, finally with my aid we pulled them apart.

' "Do sit down, sir, and have some refreshment," said Edgar. "You must be tired after your journey. Nelly prepare some tea. Would you like a curry, Mr Heathcliff?"

' "No, Mr Heathcliff does not want a curry – not yet, later on he might like some prawn samosas."

'Mr Linton stood as Cathy and Heathcliff stared passionately at each other, "It's nice to see you and Mrs Linton discussing old times," said Mr Linton.

'Mrs Linton's breast was heaving. "Heathcliff," she whispered, steam arising from her bra.

' "Cathy," responded Heathcliff, perspiration cascading down his forehead.

'"I say," said Mr Linton, "you two are getting along famously." They were too much absorbed in their mutual joy to suffer any embarrassment from Mr Linton, who sat there a gooseberry. He grew pale with annoyance when Cathy seized Heathcliff's hands again. She gave a joyous laugh. "Ahem Ahem," went Mr Linton.

'"I shall think of it as a dream tomorrow," cried Cathy. "Oh, here, Heathcliff, when you left Wuthering Heights."

'She handed him something wrapped in pink tissue paper. With his heart pounding he opened it. It was his pile ointment. Heathcliff was too full for words. They embraced.

'"Ahem Ahem," said Mr Linton. "Cathy, unless you want cold tea you best come to the table. I'm sure Mr Heathcliff will be leaving soon. Where are you staying the night? Are you going to the YMCA?"

'"No, Wuthering Heights, Mr Earnshaw invited I stay there, for some reason, he now dresses like a woman and is called Gladys."

'Mr Lockwood, I couldn't believe it, I had a presentiment that no good would come of this. Before Heathcliff left he held up his pile ointment. "Thanks for remembering, Cathy."

'"You sure you wouldn't like a quick Tandoori King Prawn?" said Edgar.

'"No thank you," said Heathcliff, loosening Cathy from his embrace, and bade us goodnight.

'In the middle of the night Mrs Linton came to my bedside. It was Cathy with the wind in her hair. "I couldn't sleep, Nelly, I want some living creature to keep me company in my happiness."

'I said, "Well, there's the dog in the kitchen."

'"No, no, Nelly, I want to talk about Heathcliff and his twelve inches, when I compare it with Edgar's, I know where my heart lies. Oh, when I think of Heath-cliff and his, my heart breaks like a hammer bomb billy bomb billy bomb bomb bomb bomb it goes, Nelly. It's terrible, I can't mention Heathcliff and his thing to Edgar. He goes into a fury. He locks himself in the bathroom and I hear him screaming as though he is stretching something and he shouts 'One day it will be bigger!'"

'I said to Miss Cathy, "It's nearly one o'clock, why don't you go for a nice five-mile barefoot run on the moors. It will calm you down and I'll be able to get some bloody sleep."

'So she ran barefooted on the moor in the wind and the rain calling out "Heathcliff, my love", and stopping now and then to pull thorns from the soles of her feet. Through all this Heathcliff was asleep with one hand on his manhood.

'Heathcliff – Mr Heathcliff I should say in future – used the liberty of visiting Thrushcross Grange cautiously at first. He used to come in various ingratiating costumes. First he came as the Pope, then Nelson, then a dustman. He tried several more until his presence was finally accepted. However, a new source of trouble came from Isabella, Linton's sister, who in a shaft of sunlight had seen swelling in Heathcliff's trousers. Her brother tried to save his sister from Heathcliff's attraction, not only her but his wife Cathy. He tried making Heathcliff sit behind a screen. When he was not there Isabella sulked, it was affecting her health, she was dwindling and fading before our eyes. We had to put a mark on her to show us where she was. One day she grew cross and, as she dwindled, rejected her breakfast, complained that the servants would not do as she told them, like jump off the roof.

'"Get back in bed," said Cathy.

'"I am in bed," said Isabella.

'"You see," said Cathy. "You're so thin we can't tell the difference."

'"You're so harsh," said Isabella.

'"How can you say I'm harsh, you naughty fondling?"

'"I'm not a naughty fondling," she shrieked, exposing herself.

'"When have I been harsh?" shrieked Cathy.

'"Yesterday," shrieked Isabella, "when we walked on the moor, while you ran barefoot with the wind and the rain through your hair with Heathcliff, you told me to ramble elsewhere."

'"No," shrieked Cathy. "I told you to bugger off." So the enmity twix sisters went on, day in day out they twixed over Heathcliff. Sometimes they even twixed *under* Heathcliff.'

Chapter XI

ONE DAY I put on my bonnet, a rock fell on my head. It was Mr Edgar's joke. "April fool," he said. The joke was on him, this was June. I made my way to Wuthering Heights. I wanted to see what this "thing" of Heathcliff's was that caused this jealousy; it caused Miss Cathy to run wild on the moors shouting "It's *mine*."

'As I drew nigh I saw a boy, it was my darling Hareton! "God bless 'ee," I said.

'He picked up a rock and threw it at my head. "April fool," he said.

'When I regained consciousness he was standing by me. "Are 'ee all right?" he said.

'I said, "Yes".

'"Then you better piss off," he said.

'"Who taught you all those evil words?"

'"That bugger Heathcliff," he said. I put an orange in his hand and bade him tell his father a woman called Nelly Dean wanted to see him.

'He stood at the door shouting "Dad". What came to the door was a woman in a blonde wig, with scarlet lips and cheeks, a green satin gown, white stockings, black mid-calf button-up boots. Lord help me, it was *Mister*

Earnshaw! Then Heathcliff came out, put his arm round Earnshaw and called him darling. And then I fainted.

'All the stress of these stormy occasions over Heathcliff gave Isabella and Cathy to contract a psychomatic itch, Isabella on the buttocks and Cathy in the groins, it was very embarrassing when they both scratched together. The next time Heathcliff came he was wearing skin-tight trousers that revealed all. Isabella was feeding some pigeons, I was standing in the kitchen window. Heathcliff went across to Isabella but, because of his tight trousers, he had to walk stiff-legged while propelling himself forward pressing his hands on his buttocks. At every step he let out a grunt of exertion. He covered the distance between Isabella and him with forty grunts. He gave her something wrapped in tissue paper tied with a pink ribbon. She opened it, it was a chapatti. She started to feed it to the pigeons, the weight of which kept them earthbound. Heathcliff looked around to see if they were alone, then he kissed her, at which Miss Isabella immediately started to scratch her buttocks. To Heathcliff it sounded like two pieces of sandpaper rubbed together. Cathy came running in barefoot fresh from the moor. "I heard scratching and thought I might help?" She pointed to Heathcliff.

'Isabella ran away to scratch herself. Heathcliff was coming across. Cathy had often come across. "Hello, Cathy," said he. "Fancy a poppadom?"

'"You must leave Isabella alone," she said scratching her own groins.

'Mr Edgar, the nerd of Thrushcross Grange came in.

'"Mr Heathcliff, I have overheard the scratching. You must leave before we all get it."

'"Try and make me," said Heathcliff." So Edgar tried

to make him. "You touch me and I'll smash your skull in," said Heathcliff.

'Three times Edgar attacked Heathcliff with fisticuffs and three times Heathcliff smashed his skull in. "Very well, if you won't leave," said Edgar, "I will"

'So saying the battered nerd went to Martell Three Star, a bargain at £8.

'"There, you're done with coming here," said Cathy, scratching the raging itch in her groin.

'Edgar told her in between scratching, "You must choose between me and Heathcliff."

'"I require to be alone," she shrieked.

'Mr Edgar bade me bring some water. I brought a jug, he threw it over her. In a few seconds she stretched herself out stiff. I whispered to Mr Edgar not to worry, how she had resolved to frighten him, by putting on a fit. He went and threw another jug of water over her. He did this several times and each time she seemed to get better.

'Next morning she came not down for breakfast.
'"Would you like some breakfast brought up?"
'"No."

'The same at lunchtime. "Would you like breakfast brought up?"
"No."

'Same at dinner. "Would you like breakfast brought up?"
"No."

'Same at tea time. "Would you like breakfast brought up?" We could hear ecstatic groans as she thought of Heathcliff and scratched her groins. Edgar heard it and thought it was somebody with a wire brush.'

Chapter XII

AFTER THREE days locked in her room, Cathy let me in to tell me she was dying, but first she finished her breakfast, eggs, bacon, kidneys and toast, then she told me again that she was dying. She lay back on her bed to show me how it was done. "Oh, I will die," she exclaimed, swallowing the last kidney. "No one cares about me," she said, finishing off the toast and marmalade. "No, wait! I've decided I will not die."

'"Very good, m'am," I said. "Is there anything you would like before you start dying again?"

'She started jumping up and down on the bed. "Where is my nerd of a husband? Has he fallen into a lethargy?"

'"Yes, m'am." I informed her he *had* fallen into a lethargy, it had taken eight of us to pull him out. "He is in the library now reading books."

'"Reading books?!!!!" she flashed. "And here I am dying."

'"Yes," I said.

'"Here I am on the brink of the grave."

'"Yes, m'am," I said. "Apart from your death, is there anything else I could bring you up on a tray, like the head of John the Baptist?"

'She stopped jumping up and down on the bed. "Does my husband know I'm dying?"

'"I'm not sure, but he has laid out his black suit."

'"Why?" she asked.

'"He says it's dead."

'"Nelly, *tell* him, tell him I am dying with the wind and the rain in my hair," she said putting white make-up on her face. She laid back and crossed her arms on her breast. "How does it look?" she asked.

'"It looks very life-like," I said. It was all I could think of saying.

'Suddenly the wind and the rain started to blow through her hair. She gave off several low moans. "Oh, Heathcliff," she moaned, scratching her groins. "They have all turned to enemies, Nelly how dreary to meet death on your own."

'"I'm sorry, m'am, when it comes to death we all have to do it on our own," I said. I watched as Cathy with her teeth tried to tear open the pillow. She whirled the pillow round and round her lovely head releasing a snow storm of feathers. She started to identify the feathers: "This is a wild duck, quack quack; this is a turkey, gobble gobble; and the pigeon, cro cro. Oh, Heathcliff! If only you were *here*."

'"Look, m'am!" I said, "you're not well, lie down and shut your eyes."

'I dragged the pillow in the direction of away for she was removing its contents by the handful. "Oh, Nelly, I have to die to make you happy."

'"Of course, m'am."

'Cathy started her jumping up and down again. "Oh, Nelly," she started. Oh fuck, I thought. "This bed", she said, "is the fairy cave under Penistone Crags and Heathcliff is with me making Chicken Tandoori. Oh, Nelly, I

long to hear the wind and the rain on my face," she said. "Open the window."

'"No, m'am, it's freezing out there."

'In one move Cathy dashed across and opened the window, leant out, then fell out. Before she had gone I grabbed one ankle and then the other, and there she hung singing and whistling. I looked down and all there was to see was snow and pubic hairs. After a long time of using all my strength I managed to pull Cathy in; she was freezing. I started to chip the ice off with a hammer.

'That moment the nerd of Thrushcross Grange staggered in; this time, it was Dewar's Black Label.

'"Miss Cathy is ill," I said.

'"You're right, Miss Cathy is ill, I'll get help," he said, and drained the bottle. "Here, let me help you chip the ice off."

'"That girl, Master Edgar, needs to run barefooted and free on the moor with the wind and the rain in her hair."

'"In her condition that would kill her," said Edgar.

'"Well, she's been talking of dying and I thought this would help," I said.

'Edgar took his timeshare dying wife in his arms and looked at her with anguish through the floating feathers.

'Cathy saw him. "Mother," she said.

'Edgar shook his head.

'"Father," said Cathy.

'Edgar shook his head.

'"Lord Horatio Nelson RN?" she said.

'"No. Cathy, it is I, Edgar."

'When she recovered consciousness, she sneered, "Ah, Ah, you have come, have you Edgar Linton?"

'"No, no," he said. "That was last night."

'Again, she semi-swooned saying, "They can't keep

me from the narrow hole in the ground, where my resting place will be 'fore the spring.''

'"I know not, master, but if I were you, I wouldn't book a double holiday for the time being.''

'"Catherine, what have you done?'' asked Edgar. Actually she had just done a butler's revenge, but it hadn't reached him yet.

'"Do you still love Heathcliff?''

'"Hush,'' said Cathy, "I want aught but him and his curries, he and I making poppadoms in the wild wind and rain on the moor; that's something you and I have never known, have we, Edgar!''

'"Her mind is wandering, sir, it could be anywhere: Lewisham, Neasden or Brixton.''

'Cathy lay scratching her groins. To deaden the sound Edgar pulled the blanket over her. "You, Nelly,'' said the nerd, "knew how ill my wife was, yet you never told me.''

'I defended myself, "Beggin' yer pardon, sir, but that is a lot of bollocks.''

'"A lot of bollocks? How many would you say?'' said Edgar.

'"I have no idea how many, I was just guessing.''

'At that moment Cathy started clucking like a chicken.

'"My wife is having an attack of chicken,'' said Edgar. "Has this happened before?''

'"Oh, yes,'' I said. "It's usually followed by an attack of duck.'' My warning was too late as Cathy already started to quack.

'"There, there, dear,'' said Edgar.

'She struggled to free herself from his loving embrace, then she started to moo.

'"Nelly, this woman needs help.''

' "Yes, master, shall I get a doctor?"

'Outside a terrible shock: someone had hanged Miss Isabella's dog on a hook in the wall with a handkerchief. I thought it strange, you don't often see a dog hanging on a wall. While untying the knot, it seemed to me I repeatedly caught the beat of horses' hooves galloping at some distance. I was so right, what I heard was indeed the beat of horses' hooves galloping at some distance.

'Fortunately Dr Kenneth was just issuing from the home of a patient he had killed. "How are things at Thrushcross?" he asked.

' "Well, that Heathcliff rides in to court Miss Isabella," I said.

' "Oh," said Dr Kenneth, pausing to pick up a few leeches he'd dropped. "Does she give him the cold shower?"[1] he asked.

' "No, it's quite warm," I said.

'When Dr Kenneth arrived at Cathy she was sleeping, exhausted by her farmyard impressions.

' "Yes," said Dr Kenneth. "She has been suffering from farmyard impressions, and that will be fifty pounds."

' "Oh," said Edgar, "Isn't that a bit much?"

' "Yes," said Dr Kenneth. "That's why I ask for it."

' "Supposing she has another outbreak of farmyard impressions?"

' "Then", said Dr Kenneth, "send for the vet."

'Then a terrible shock, the maid had found Miss Isabella's bed empty! "She's gone, sir," she told nerd of Thrushcross Grange.

' "Gone!" he said, and struck a dramatic pose. "She's

---

[1] Some kind of sexual ritual. *Ed.*

gone." It didn't do much except give him tennis elbow at that painful moment.

'Heathcliff and Isabella were getting married.'

Chapter XIII

OR TWO MONTHS, there was no news of Isabella and Heathcliff who were on honeymoon in a bed at the YMCA. Meantime, Greenwich meantime, Cathy was getting over being a lunatic. Ever since her recovery, Dr Kenneth had cancelled all the farm feed she'd been eating: oats, bran, grass, hay, chicken feed and duck mash. On the first day of Cathy's recovery Edgar had put on her pillow a handful of golden crocuses. She ate them. "Those were the earliest flowers at Heights," she said. "I shall never be there, but once more," said the lunatic, "and then you'll leave me, and I shall remain for ever."

'"Despite that Linton lavished his kindest caresses and a few quick gropes. They sat her by the fire in the parlour. To entertain her Edgar blacked up as a minstrel, he sang her minstrel songs, he played her the tambourine, he played the banjo. Then washing it all off – he came on as a gypsy. He did a gypsy dance round the fire, he played the violin, then as a Russian he did dances. Through all this Cathy slept peacefully.

'I got a letter from Isabella:

Dear Nelly
I am here in Wuthering Heights. A question I ask

you — Is Heathcliff a man, or a devil? With
that thing I don't know how he gets his trousers
on.

I have met Hareton, Edgar's nephew. At first I
thought he was a clothes horse so ragged he was. I
said 'Hello, Hareton darling, can I give you a kiss?'
'No, bugger off,' he said. 'I'm your aunty, darling,'
I said. 'Throttler, see her? Get her boy!' Hareton
said, prodding a bull pit terrier, whereupon I fled
outside.

I knocked on an outside door. It was opened by a
man wearing a beautiful body-clinging velvet dress
trimmed with white fur, his face was heavily made
up. 'Oh,' he said disappointingly. 'I was hoping for
a sailor.' 'I am Mrs Heathcliff,' I said. The man
clenched his fists. 'One day I'll kill him,' he said.
'Could I have a date in advance?' I said. 'Monday
12 August,' he said.

So, Nelly, I sit and wait, sometimes I stand and
wait. I hate Heathcliff. I tell you, Nelly, never let a
big one fool you.

                                        Isabella.

'I showed the letter to Master Edgar, he looked in the
envelope to see if there were any postal orders. I asked
him to forgive her.

'"Forgive? Never!" he shouted. "All she can have is
this Eccles cake." Mr Edgar's coldness depressed me,
about five inches.

'So, as a dwarf, I set off with the precious Eccles cake
for Wuthering Heights. When I got there I entered
without knocking. Normally quite loud knocking ema-
nates from me. Inside there was never such a dirty
dreary scene. If it had been me I would have swept the

hearth, dusted the table and legs. Then in came Isabella,
her face hadn't been swept, her legs were all dusty, her
hair hung down full of cobwebs. Heathcliff was there.
"Come, pull up a chair and sit down."

'I shook my head. "No, I'd rather stand," I said.

'"Very well, pull up a chair and stand on it," he said.

'"Isabella, m'am," I said, "Mr Edgar sent you this."

'"Oh," said Isabella with tears in her eyes. "An Eccles
cake." She took it and pressed it to her breast, nursing it
like a baby. "Look, Heathcliff, an Eccles cake," she said.

'Heathcliff took it and ate it. Then, putting one hand
behind his bottom, he said in a strained voice, "Just
pushing 'em back in. Look, Nelly, we don't want you
to go back empty-handed. Here, here is a six-inch nail.
Put it in your bag. I'm sure you'll find a use for it."

'I told him that Mr Edgar would not allow him to see
Cathy. "He says you must leave England and go to the
land of your curry."

'Heathcliff was trying to go white with rage, but
could only manage cream. "It seems," he said, "your
master should have nothing but humanity and sense of
duty to fall back on."

'"No," I said. "As far as I know the only thing he's
got to fall back on is the floor."

'Heathcliff shot his hands in his pockets and moved
the bulge. "I *will* see Cathy," he shouted. "She's still
good for a few weekends in Brighton." He paused, then
said, "Yes, I was a fool to fancy for the moment that she
valued Linton's attachment more than mine, though I
haven't used my attachment since the honeymoon." He
then took the dog, Throttler, and threw him out of the
window. "It's time for his walk," he said. Then walking
back and forth, forth and back – once he just went forth
and forth and didn't come back – he said, "If ever

Linton did anything to Cathy, I'd tear his heart out and drink his blood."

'"You can't," I said. "He's Rhesus negative."

'"Blast," he said.

'"Any encounter between you and the master would kill her altogether."

'"Kill her altogether? Rubbish!" he said. "Her legs might go numb but that will soon wear off. Just plunge them into hot water."

'Isabella came to me. "Did you bring nothing from Linton save an Eccles cake?" she asked.

'"Nothing," I replied. "That's why my basket is empty except a six-inch nail." Isabella returned to her corner to do haddock-stretching for supper.

'"Let me tell you, Mr Heathcliff, by now Cathy has forgotten you."

'"Arggh, no! Nelly," he said. "You know as well as I do, for every thought she spends on Linton, she spends a thousand on me. I am 999 thoughts ahead of him." He threw Isabella a fresh haddock to stretch. "Two words," he said. "Two words would explain my life without Cathy. Two words: death and hell."

'"That's three words," I said.

'As he stood with his back to the fire. There came a burning smell. The back of his trousers was scorching. "Tush!" he said, beating out the fire on the back of his trousers. "Listen Nelly, Linton is no degree dearer to Cathy than her dog or her horse, her chicken, or duck."

'In a fit of pique, Isabella threw her haddock to the ground. "Catherine and Edgar love each other even though they don't often do it," she said.

'"Tush, woman, get on with your haddock-stretch-ing," he snarled.

'I spoke to him sternly. "Mrs Heathcliff is used to the

life of gentle lady, brought up to do bugger-all all day."

'"Listen to this, Nelly," he said. "Isabella, do you really *hate* me? If I let you alone for an hour, wouldn't you come sighing and wheedling to me. My God, Nelly, only yesterday she wheedled at me for three hours! In the end she suffered wheedle withdrawals, *and* she's not even a good shag. All she says is when are you going to stop, it's breakfast time."

'"That's no good, Mr Heathcliff, you must treat her like a lady every morning. She should be dusted and polished."

'"You see, Nelly," he said, "I only love her from the waist down."

'Isabella leapt to her feet, letting another partially stretched haddock fall to the floor. "He's a monster, Nelly, he treasures his pile ointment more than me. His real love is Cathy. Just mention her name and he gets a swelling."

'"That's enough," shouted Heathcliff. Great waves of garlic, curry and karachi wafted from him. Grabbing Isabella he shook her till her teeth rattled, her shoes fell off and her knickers came down. "Upstairs with you, prepare to continue the honeymoon."

'"Do you know what *pity* means?" I said, hastening to resume my bonnet.

'"Stop," he said. "Do not resume that bonnet!"

'"Please stay out of curry-smelling distance," I said.

'"So, Nelly," he said from another room. "I am determined to see Catherine again."

'At the mention of her name I noticed the swelling in his trousers. Using money, he forced me to take a note to Cathy and a freshly stretched haddock. Notwithstanding my journey hither was sadder than my journey thither. On my way thither I was happy but coming hither I was sad. I tried to avoid hither and arrived back via thither.'

Chapter XIV

I HAD MADE UP my mind not to give Cathy Heathcliff's letter until Mr Linton was somewhere else, like China. This day Cathy, in a pure white dress save a few gravy stains, was seated in a chair at the window; her long thick hair which had been partly removed during her illness was now back from the cleaners and hung in tresses down her back, her haggard aspect had gone; she had a peculiar expression arising from her mental state. She gave chicken clucks and an occasional quack quack. It stamped her as one doomed to decay — already bits were falling off her. A book lay spread before her, she had been eating it. It had been placed there with loving hand by Edgar. Gimmerton chapel bells were still ringing, their sound came soothingly to the ear, sometimes it reached the teeth and up the nose.

'"There's a letter for you, Cathy, shall I open it?"

'"Yes," she answered.

'Taking a hammer I smashed the seal to pieces. I opened it. "It's very short," I said.

'"Is it from a dwarf?" she said. As she read the letter her face came alive with passion and an attack of the hiccups. "Where is he — hic?," she said.

'"He's outside by the tree," I said.

'As she spoke I observed a large dog lying on the sunny grass. He raised his ears and started to bark when he got a kick up the arse from Heathcliff.

'"What – hic – was that?" asked Cathy.

'"It was Heathcliff kicking a dog up the arse," I said.

'"Ooh, how lovely," she said, hicking and clapping her hands together. Cathy listened and gazed towards the entrance of her chamber.

'He did not hit the right room directly, but walked by mistake into the toilet shouting, "Darling." Finally he came in; in a stride or two he was at her side and had grasped her in his arms, and before I could stop them they'd had a couple of quickies. He neither spoke nor loosened his hold for five minutes. He rained burning hot kisses, and steam started to issue from Cathy's clothes; her shoes melted.

'"Oh Cathy! O my life! I can't bear it." It was the first sentence he uttered in a strained voice, due to the pressure in his trousers, and before I could stop them they had another couple of quickies.

'"Not so fast," gasped Cathy. "Pretend it's timeshare."

'I threw a bucket of water over them but it was no use.

'"What now," said Cathy. "Oh, Heathcliff. You", she said, "and Edgar have broken my heart."

'"Oh, I am sorry," said Heathcliff.

'"You have killed me," she said.

'"Oh?" said Heathcliff. "Are you dead?"

'"How many years do you mean to live after I am gone?" she said.

'"About sixty, if it's all right with you." Heathcliff knelt on one knee to embrace her. He attempted to rise, but she seized his hair and kept him down. "I wish I could hold you till we were both dead."

' "Well, you go first," said Heathcliff.

' "Tell me, Heathcliff," she said, shaking her head, "why shouldn't you suffer? I do."

' "I do suffer, Cathy, I have piles," he said. "Don't torture me, Cathy, till I'm as mad as yourself." So saying, he wrenched his head free. A tuft of hair came away in her hand, leaving him with a bald patch.

' "Will you say twenty years hence, that's the grave of Cathy Earnshaw?" she asked.

' "If you want me to, I'll say that's the grave of Cathy Earnshaw."

'She hissed and spat at him.

' "Are you possessed by the devil?" he asked.

' "No," she said. "The Bradford and Bingley." She lay back, her heart beating wildly — bonk bonk bonkity bonk. "Come, Heathcliff, and kneel down again," she said.

'As he did there came a loud cracking from the arthritis in his knees. Heathcliff stood up and went to the back of her chair and leaned over her. She could see right up his nose. "Oh, no," she whispered as he walked to the fireplace, where he stood, silent with his back to the fire.

'Due to the heat in his trousers they caught fire. In a fury of sparks and swearing he beat out the flames, encouraged by Cathy's shouting. "Go, man, go!" She gave a low moan. "I'm tired of being enclosed in here. I want to escape barefoot on to the moor and let the wind and rain blow through my hair," she said.

' "But, Miss Cathy," I said, "the last time you did that, you got pneumonia, remember?"

' "Yes, it was wonderful!" she said. She gave me her hand to hold, it was getting too heavy for her. "Nelly," she said. "You are more fortunate than I, you in full health and strength."

'"Nay, m'am, I have varicose veins," I said.

'"Oh," said Cathy softly, "I wish I were well enough to have those." Suddenly she had an attack of chicken, she started clucking. Heathcliff, his trousers still smouldering, went across to soothe her. In her eagerness she arose, supporting herself on her zimmer. He turned to her looking absolutely desperate, his eyes aflame with passion. Her breasts heaved convulsively. He gave them a quick squeeze; an instance they held asunder. Suddenly Cathy made a spring. He caught her and they were locked together long enough for another couple of quickies. That done, he dropped her to the floor with a thud! He flung himself into the nearest seat. When I went to pick Cathy up, he gnashed at me, gnash! gnash! and foamed at me like a mad dog. "Here, boy," I said and threw him a bone. He leaned over her. She put her hand up to clasp his neck and bring her cheek to his. He covered her with frantic caresses and groping, stopping only to gnaw the bone.

'"Yes," he said, "you loved me. What right have you to leave me, eh? eh? eh? eh? Why did you eh? eh? eh? eh? Why did you fall for that creep Edgar Linton eh? eh? eh? eh? eh? eh? eh? eh?"

'"Let me alone," sobbed Cathy. "If I've done wrong, I'm dying for it, isn't that enough?"

'"It's hard to look in those eyes to forgive and feel those wasted boobs," said Heathcliff, weeping floods of tormented tears. It was in moments like this he longed for Prawn Madras.

'They were silent, their faces against each other, crying. At least I suppose the weeping was on both sides, that is their tears ran down each other's back. I could hear church bells ringing. "Service is over," I said.

'"Yes," said Heathcliff, "I've given her a good service."

'"My master will be home soon," I said.

'Heathcliff groaned a curse, "Awwwgfuck!" he said.

'I could see Mr Linton staggering in through the gate, pissed from the Black Bull.

'"Do be quick," I said to Heathcliff.

'"I must go, Cathy," he said, pulling up his trousers. "I won't stay five yards from your window," he said.

'"How many will you stay then?" asked Cathy, pulling him back by his braces.

'He strained away till the braces stretched across the room, then Cathy released them and they hit Heathcliff a sickening thwack!

'"Oh, dear," cursed an enraged Heathcliff. Taking up a starting position of a runner, he dashed across to embrace Cathy; she grabbed his hair, pulling out two more tufts; he was now nearly bald. She lay back with the wind and rain in her hair. "Don't go, don't go." There was a mad resolution on her face and down one side of her body. "No," she shrieked, "I shall die, I shall die tiddly, I tie tiddly I tie."

'"She does not know what she says," I said.

'"Neither do I," said Heathcliff.

'"This is the most diabolical deed you ever did," I said.

'"No," he said, "I once set fire to a cat."

'As Mr Edgar approached I said, "We are done for, master, mistress, servants."

'"Oh, no," said Heathcliff, "I only done the mistress, I'm not into serial sex."

'Mr Edgar came in, his face blanched blanch. He sprang at Heathcliff, missed and crashed to the floor and was sick on the carpet. What he meant to do I cannot tell. Getting up from his sick, he said, "Heathcliff, unless you be a – hic – fiend, help her first – hic – then you shall – hic – speak to me," he said addressing the hat stand. He staggered into the parlour and sat down with Vat 69 at £2 a bottle. With great difficulty and after resorting to many means, including relief massage, we managed to restore Cathy to sensation, but she moaned and knew nobody, not even Queen Victoria or Gladstone. Repeatedly we asked her, "Who is Queen Victoria or Glandstone?" but it was no use. I then asked Heathcliff if he could leave. "Please piss off."

' "Very well," he said, "I'll be in the garden, I'll use a tree."

'He sent a rapid glance through the half open door of the chamber and ascertaining that what I stated was apparently true, delivered the house of his luckless presence.'[1]

---

[1] Descriptive writing at its best. *Ed.*

Chapter XVI

THAT WEEK, Cathy died, she was laid out in the parlour. Edgar Linton had his head laid on the pillow and bloody uncomfortable it was. Cathy lay on her bier: no angel could appear more beautiful, more dead. I went to tell Heathcliff. He was among the trees. He leaned against the old chestnut tree. He had been standing a long time in that position, and was heavily crippled by it.

'"She's dead," he said. "Put your handkerchief away, don't snivel before me," he said.

'"I didn't know it was your turn," I said. A foolish notion struck me that his heart was sad. His lips moved as in prayer. Actually he was chewing betel-nut, his gaze bent on the ground. He was looking for conkers.

'"Yes, she's dead," I said.

'"How did she die?"

'"Lying down," I said.

'"That's a good position for it," he said. "Did she mention me?" he added.

'"How could she, she was dead," I said. "Her senses never returned – she recognized nobody, not even Queen Victoria, even though we held photographs," I said.

'Suddenly in a rage he said, "Damn you, Cathy Linton," and stamped his foot on the root of a tree, bruising his Achilles' tendon. He leaped around holding the injured member. In time to it I clapped hands and sang a hornpipe.

'I told him, "Her last words were 'The sausages are burning.'"

'Tears came to his eyes, but they were for his Achilles' tendon. There was a pause as he gobbed out his betel-nut. "Cathy Linton, you said, 'I killed you,' then haunt me, preferably on Saturdays between nine and twelve." He dashed his head against the knotted trunk, bruising his Achilles' tendon. "Damn you, Cathy Linton," he said, dashing his head. "Damn you, Achilles' tendon," he said, feeling a lump on his Achilles' tendon. He looked up and howled like a wolf. Hearing this, the house dog galloped out and attacked him, only to have his arse kicked again.

'After this I returned to the home where Cathy lay in state. Her coffin was open – to let the wind and the rain in – and strewn with flowers. Linton spent long nights sleeping by the coffin. It made no difference, for in the morning she was still dead. Outside, Heathcliff was making his curry and sleeping by the trees. I was conscious of his desire to enter. So when Linton was sleeping off Dow's Crusted Port 1840, I left the window to Cathy's coffin open. He apparently came in, retrieved the tufts of his hair she had in her hands and left; so silently had he come, it was only the smell of curry that told of his presence, that and £15 missing from the tea caddy.

'Mr Earnshaw turned down the invitation to the funeral, saying he hadn't a suitable dress, and hadn't finished dancing with his sailor "Shagger" MacGee. The funeral passed off peacefully.'

Chapter XV

*N*OW MY MASTER, Mr Linton, keeps to his room. I took possession of the lonely parlour, converting it into a nursery, and there I was sitting with a moaning doll of a child laid out on my knee, with me powdering its "particulars". The child was Cathy's, born just before she died.[1] She was called Catherine.

'Suddenly the door burst open and some person entered, out of breath and laughing: "Ha ha ha ha ha ha ha haha."

'"How dare, how dare you, ha ha ha ha ha ha ha haha in here? What would Mr Linton say?"

'"Excuse me," said a familiar voice. "Nothing, Mr Linton is in bed, pissed, ha ha ha ha ha ha ha ha haha." With that the speaker came forward to the fire. "Ha ha ha ha ha ha ha ha ha," it went. "I've run all the way from Wuthering Heights ha ha ha ha haha." The ha ha'ing intruder was Isabella Heathcliff. She certainly was in no laughing predicament. She was soaked to the skin and the skin soaked to the bone. She wore a young dress, befitting her age, not her position. When she changed into dry clothing she came and sat down. "You

---

[1] A bit late in the book to tell this. *Ed.*

sit opposite me," she said, "and put poor Catherine's baby away."

'I rang the bell and handed the child to a servant. "Drown it," I said.

'She told me she had run away from Heathcliff. It was a good direction to go in. She mentioned that she couldn't stand another curry-filled love-making. "He uses a chapatti as a contraceptive! I hate him, I've recovered from my desire to be killed by him."

' "That's very sensible of you," I said.

' "At first he said he was besotted with me. I don't want to besot anybody."

' "Hush, hush," I said. "Be more charitable, there are worse men than he is."

' "Oh, really?" she said, cheering up. "Where?"

' "Luton," I said.

'She went on, "He's a monster, you know what he did to me last night?"

' "No," I said.

' "Thank heaven for that," she said, closing her eyes in memory of the horror. "Heathcliff destroyed my love, he also hurt his Achilles' tendon. I have no power to feel for him, now he has feel on his own," said Isabella.

'She told me that every night since Cathy died, Heathcliff had come here and slept in the woods. "It's a wonder," she said, "it's a wonder that Edgar didn't call a constable and hand him into police custard!"[2] At Wuthering Heights she told me that these days she wasn't so fearful of Heathcliff or his chapatti. "I move up and down the house, less with the foot of a frightened thief, than formerly."

'She told me she had a cupboard full of feet from

[2] Typist's error.

frightened thieves. She recounted to me of a terrible evening. She was by the fire, Earnshaw sat in his evening-gown, sipping port and lemon in between putting on make-up. There was a knock at the door, it was Heathcliff. "Ahhh," screamed Earnshaw. "'Tis Heathcliff, I'll kill him," he said, taking a pistol from his stocking top.

'Isabella ran to the window and warned Heathcliff. "You better seek shelter somewhere else tonight, like Belgium. Mr Earnshaw has a mind to kill you."

'"You cow, you better open the door, I'm *not* going to Belgium," he raged.

'"Come in and get shot then."

'Heathcliff burst into the room, it went all over the floor. Before Earnshaw could kill him, Heathcliff knocked the pistol and handbag from Earnshaw's grasp.

'"I'll tell my boyfriend about you," sobbed Earnshaw. "You half killed me," he said from the live half. He replaced his dress straps over his lovely shoulders.

'"Not a word of this to anyone," said Heathcliff. "Not even Mrs Gladys Noff of No. 22 Gabriel Street, Honor Oak Park, SE26."

'"I'll not hold my tongue," Isabella said.

'"All right," he said, "hold this," and gave her a banana.

'Earnshaw rose from the floor picking up his teeth scattered around.

'Next morning Earnshaw came down, wearing a pink satin gown with roses at the waist and black patent shoes. He looked beautiful. How lucky his sailor boyfriend "Shagger" MacGee was. Then Heathcliff arrived, "his forehead," Isabella said, "that I once thought manly," was shaded with a heavy cloud, a cold wind and slight rainfall on the north side; his face was one of unspeakable sadness.

'"Your face is one of unspeakable sadness," Isabella said. "Oh, Nelly," she continued, "I owe him so much, it's about three pounds five shillings. On only one condition can I forgive him, it's an eye for an eye, a tooth for a tooth, a leg for a leg, an ear for an ear, an Achilles' tendon for an Achilles' tendon."

'"Stop, miss," I said. "There won't be much of him left!"

'Hindley wanted some water. So I threw a glass over him. Isabella stopped talking, thank Christ. She took a drink of tea. She said goodbye. I begged her to stay longer. "I'm five foot six, isn't that long enough?" she said. I pleaded with her to stay, but she turned a deaf ear, she also turned the sound one, alternating between the two: it sounded as if she was coming and going at the same time.

'She boarded her coach and went to live at some address in London. There she gave birth to a son, called Linton. He was an ailing peevish creature with a cough like a horse, which made the mother happy as she loved horse. I said Mrs Heathcliff lived about a dozen years – actually it was eleven so it was about, as I say, a dozen years after quitting her husband, she had frequently quitted him, his body was one mass of quitmarks. She and Edgar Linton both lacked the ruddy health that you generally meet in these parts. The people's parts around here are all ruddy. What her illness was is uncertain: some say an elephant charged her and gave her elephanti-tis. Before she died, she wrote to Edgar to inform him of how she had suffered from elephants, also instructions on how he must adopt her son, Linton, along with a recipe for jam rolls and lentil cake. The letter was eighty-six pages long. It took Edgar seven days to read it. At the bottom a PS read: "Please come and see me, bring the jam rolls, lentil cake and anti-elephant cream. Hurry, I am dying!" In a frenzy, Edgar spent the next two days making the rolls and cake. Then leaving young Catherine in my charge,[3] he left for London by walking stick. He was a mean man. He was away three weeks, two he spent getting there. I remained behind with of which more anon.[4]

'Mr Heathcliff met me in the village one day, inquired where she lived. I refused to tell. I put it like this: "Fuck off." Another time he asked me about the infant. I put it like this: "Fuck off," I said with a grim smile. He mounted his horse and fucked off. Then Isabella died. She died from deafness: there was this steamroller coming up behind her and she didn't hear it. That was twelve years ago. We come now to Mr Edgar Linton, still pissed and mourning for Cathy; he shunned conversation and was fit for discussing nothing. The death of Cathy transformed him, he threw up his office of magistrate. It crashed three miles away. He missed Cathy, so in memory of her he invested in a life-size rubber doll. I used to draw comparisons between Linton and Earnshaw. Linton recalled Cathy's memory with ardent alcoholism and the rubber doll.

'One day Dr Kenneth arrived. He stepped off his horse into a pile of it. "Guess who's given us the slip now, do you think?" the delighted doctor said.

'"Mrs Gladys Noffs at No. 22 Gabriel Street?" I said hopefully.

[3] Her charge was two shillings an hour plus VAT. *Ed*.
[4] More anon to come. *Ed*.

'"Guess again," said the cheery doctor, "and nip up the corner of your apron.[5] I'm certain you'll need it."

'So I nipped up the corner of my apron[6] but I told him I didn't need to. "Who has snuffed it?" I asked.

'"It's Earnshaw," said the cheery doctor.

'"Why do you sound so happy?" I asked.

'"Because", he said, "it wasn't me. He died of the drink, he fell in it and drowned."

'Poor Mr Earnshaw, I couldn't help missing him, though he had the worst tricks a man can imagine. He could do the white-eared elephant and the last turkey in the shop! I had only heard how lonely soldiers used to do these tricks to entertain each other.

'I went to Wuthering Heights to see Earnshaw laid out. I had seen him laid out before, but only face down, but this was my last chance to see him again. I saw poor Earnshaw laid out surrounded by empty bottles. The fumes were everywhere; no one dared strike a match or he would have exploded. When he died he'd been wearing his lovely off-the-shoulder white gown. Except for the egg down the front, Earnshaw in his white gown looked lovely in his coffin. I thought, did this man *really* do the last turkey in the shop? Alcohol had preserved him so well. It seemed a shame to bury him, but any minute he might explode, and as it was coming on to rain and we didn't want to get him wet, we put him under.

'Heathcliff was now *master* of Wuthering Heights! He had also against his wishes inherited Hareton whom he weaned off roast beef and two veg on to Chicken Vindaloo. He also kept him for occasional hitting.'

[5] Totally baffling. *Ed*.
[6] Even more baffling. *Ed*.

Chapter XVI

CATHY'S CHILD, Catherine, was now thirteen, and grew like a larch, which is in the direction of up, she had the Earnshaws' dark eyes, but the Linton's small features, some so small you could hardly see them. People would look at her face and say, "What is that?"

'She would say, "It's a small feature." Her capacity for attachments reminded me of her mother, who always kept a drawer full of attachments for when Heathcliff came. If a servant vexed her, she'd tell her father, "I've been vexed," and her father would go and kill the servant.

'Till she reached the age of thirteen, she had never been beyond the range of the park by herself. Mr Linton would take her on a lead. Sometimes he would let her run with the lead off. If any men drew near, he'd put a false beard and moustache on the girl and cover her body with a blanket – even then a lesbian proposed to her.

'"Nelly," she asked. "How long will it be before I can walk on top of these hills off the lead? What's on the other side?"

'"The other side is, well, the other side," I said.

'"And," she said, "what are those golden rocks like when you stand under them?"

'"They're like golden rocks, Catherine," I said. I could have said they were regional branches of Lloyds Bank, but what good would it have done?

'One day after breakfast Catherine vanished. I asked the gardener if he had seen her. He said, "Yes, she has ridden away on her pony along with two pointers. She was a-laughing ha-ha, so was the horse and the pointers. They all galloped out of sight, after that I couldn't see them." I went searching for her. She might have been killed clambering among the rocks or broken her bones like the radius, the ulna, the tibia and the fibia, the humerus, the metacarples, the coxyx. Then I came upon Charlie, one of the pointers. He was pointing nor-nor-east. I ran to the door, knocking vehemently. A woman answered the door vehemently. "Are you looking for your young mistress and her laughing horse? She's in the big house, Wuthering Heights!"

'I felt my blood run cold, then it walked lukewarm, then ran hot again. I entered and there was my young mistress seated on the earth and by her lay the other pointer, pointing due south. There was Hareton, now eighteen, who stared at her, not comprehending her witty talk or silver laughter: all the lad wanted was a shag.

'"Miss," I said, "put your hat on and home at once!"

'"What do you mean?" she asked.

'"Hur-Hur-Hur," went Hareton. "Dats fune-ee Hur Hur Hur."

'"Put the home on and hat at once," I said: it still didn't sound right.

'"Hur Hur Hur," laughed Hareton, who only wanted a shag.

'I said, "Home hat and put on." It was getting worse.

'In a temper Catherine stamped her foot – unfortunately on the dog's tail — the dog bolted and shot out of the back door, nor-nor-east.

'"Now, now," I said to her, "let us have no petulance."

'"Let us have no petulance," she repeated. "What's wrong with having no petulance? It doesn't harm anybody. I've had no petulance. It doesn't harm anybody. I've had no petulance many times and it's never affected me," she said, stamping her foot where the dog's tail used to be. "Oh, dear, he's gone," she said sadly.

'"Put the hat on at home at once!" I said, getting less articulate by the minute. "Miss Catherine, if you were aware whose house this was, you'd be glad to leave," I said.

'"It's your father's, isn't it?" said Catherine to Hareton.

'"Dur no hes nod my farder," said the lad.

'"Oh, then," said Catherine, "you must be a servant."

'At this remark Hareton grew black as thunder.

'"Look," said Catherine, "he's about to start raining."

'"Damn you, you saucy witch," said Hareton with cutting wit.

'"I'm sorry to tell you this," I said. "This lad is your cousin."

'At this she grabbed her throat, and gasped, "No, not this idiot," and fainted to the floor with a sickening thud.

'"Der, O'im zorry O offended 'ee," said Hareton, and threw a bucket of water over her. He was quite a well-built lad, used to lounging on the moors after rabbits, grouse and kangaroos, but mostly he wanted a shag. At times the heat in his trousers was unbearable, so it was

necessary to put leeches and weights on him to reduce
the swelling.

'Contrite, he brought Catherine's high-spirited pony
to the back door, which was unfortunate as she had
gone to the front one. Finally, she mounted her high-
spirited pony. She gave a cheery wave as her high-
spirited pony lashed out, breaking Hareton's left leg.
Accompanied by her two pointers facing due south, she
departed for home leaving me to return on my own.

'Alas! on the way back both the pointers died of dog
flu'. There had been a spate of it on the moors. What
happened was that the dog would give a sudden cough,
lie on its back with its legs in the air, give a low growl
and snuff it.

'When I got back to Thrushcross Grange, I was
exhausted. Catherine was in her nightdress, sitting by
the fire reading the Bible — how Zachariah went to
heaven in a fiery chariot with third-degree burns.'

Chapter XIX

A LETTER EDGED in black was waiting. It announced the master's forthcoming return. He wrote bidding me go into mourning for his sister. Immediately I blacked out my teeth. I started practising crying as soon as I could. I tried saying "Boo hoo hoo" a few times. Catherine ran wild with joy at the idea of welcoming back her father. Mile after mile she ran wild with joy across the moors like her mother. She ran up the hill and down the dale. She ran gasping. When wild with joy she came to a halt. "Is he back yet?" she gasped.

'"No," I said, and off she went, running wild with joy mile after mile. Her father had better arrive soon or she'd never last out. After sixty miles, we made her stop.

'The evening of the father's expected arrival came but the coach was late, it had malaria, so off Catherine went on another joyous run. By then the father was drawing nigh. He drew nigh seven times till he finally arrived back. Since early morning, she had been busy with her own small affairs — the milkman, the baker and the butcher's boy. She was now attired in her new black deep mourning dress, she was so happy! Poor thing, her aunt's death impressed her with no definite sorrow. She

herself had said, "My aunt's death has impressed me
with no definite sorrow."

'I told her that, along with her father, was coming her
cousin Linton. "Oh, how lovely," she said. "We can show
him where the dogs are buried." Linton's mother had
sent Edgar a lock of Linton's hair; the boy was half bald
for months. "Oh, I am happy," said Catherine. "Oh,
papa, dear dear papa. Come, Nelly, let's run, come run."
She ran and returned and ran again many times before I
reached the gate. "Ah," she exclaimed, "I see some dust
on the road – they are coming."

'The dust arrived but there was no one in it. Obviously
they were not travelling by dust. Then a travelling carriage
with malaria rolled into sight; the horse gave me a big
welcoming smile. Miss Cathy shrieked, stood in the road,
arms outstretched and the coach ran over her. She was
shaken but not stirred or hurt. Her father, pissed, fell out the
coach in a heap of dust on the floor. Cathy took him in
her arms, "Oh, daddy, daddy," she sang.

'"Who are you?" he said, taking a swig from a flask.

'I explained to him who Cathy was.

'"Good Lord, wonderful news, I've had a daughter,
without a wife, a male immaculate conception."

'Then her cousin Linton emerged, wearing a wig. He
was a boy of eleven or a girl of twelve. It turned out to
be the former.

'"Ah," said Cathy, "you've turned out to be the former
boy of eleven. Come, let us run!"

'I cautioned Cathy that her cousin was not so strong
and merry as she was. I told her that he was in fact a
miserable little bastard, and I added that he had lost his
mother.

'"Then we must look for her," said Cathy.

'"This is your cousin, Cathy, Linton," I said, putting

their little hands together, but he took his little hand away, the little creep.

'"There, there, you'll soon get used to her and she'll take you running wild with joy," I said.

'I took the boy into the house. I thought the change would do him good, seeing this innocent boy awoke a deep primitive instinct in me: it was manual strangulation.

'All of us entered the house and mounted to the library where we dismounted and had tea. We placed Linton on a chair where he burst into tears. "I cannot sit on a chair," he bawled.

'"Then what do you sit on?" said Master Edgar.

'"My mother's knee," he wailed.

'Alas! we didn't have a mother's knee handy so we sat him on the sofa, which was soft like his mother's knee.

'"Fancy," said Master Edgar. "His mother had a knee like a sofa."

'After a cup of tea the lad cheered up. Sometimes he cheered sideways and downwards but mostly up.

'"Oh, he'll do well," said the master to me.

'"He'll do well at what?" I said.

'"Well," said the master, "he might take after his mother and die." That was one of the master's jokes. They'd said Edgar Linton killed ninety-nine per cent of all known jokes.

'I had seen Linton to bed. I was downstairs lighting a candle, when a maid told me Joseph was waiting at the door. He had been waiting by the window till I discovered his mistake.

'"I shall ask him what he wants first," I said. I opened the door, he wasn't there.

'"I've discovered my mistake," he said coming in the window.

'"What do you want?" I asked coldly. It was terrible news: Heathcliff had sent him to fetch Linton to *Wuthering Heights*!!!

'When Master Edgar Linton heard the news, he was thunderstruck–how thunder got into so small a room is a mystery. Thank Heaven lightning doesn't strike twice in the same place. There and then the lightning then struck him in the same place. He took a great gulp of Martell's brandy, a bargain at eighteen shillings a bottle. I watched his Adam's apple going up and down like a yo-yo. An expression of exceeding great sorrow overcast his features. Indeed even his eyebrows looked heart-broken. Again he resorted to the eighteen shillings a bottle and pocket billiards, then spoke to Joseph. "The boy will stay here tonight."

'I told him Joseph wasn't in the room yet. I admitted the old man.

'"Tell Mister Heathcliff his schon hic schall come hic to–morrish ahhh."

'Joseph in a rage banged his stick on the floor, breaking it in two; using one half (and therefore bent double) he left the room.

'"That's got hic rid of him," said Master Edgar who then broke terrible wind that rattled the windows and pictures fell off the wall. "Ah, that's got rid of that," he said. In fact it got rid of everybody.'

Chapter XX

IT WAS FIVE o'clock next morning. Young Linton was reluctant to be aroused from his bed, he was reluctant to be aroused from under his bed, reluctant to be aroused from the chair by his bed, or hanging out of the window by his bed. The hammer on his fingers released them. He fell into the water butt in the garden. Later, by standing on his chest, we made him eat breakfast. "My father?" he cried in strange perplexity. "Mamma never told me I had a father in strange perplexity."

'"No," I said. "Your mother was waiting till you were twenty-one so you could stand the shock of knowing you had one."

'"Was he ever struck twice by lightning?" he asked.

'"No," I said. "That was your uncle."

'"Will anyone come with me to meet my father?" said the boy.

'"I shall be your companion," I said. At the mention of that he fell into a brown study; it took us three hours to get him out. When we rode off to see Heathcliff at Wuthering Heights, I told him Uncle Edgar and Cathy and Mrs Gladys Noffs would visit him. The bright sunshine and the gentle canter of the horse relieved his despondency. He suddenly gave a strain and a grunt.

'"Ah, that's better, I've just relieved myself of my despondency," he said. "What's my father like?" he asked. I should have said "women". But, no, I said. "He's got black hair and eyes and he's brown." I did not think it wise to mention the huge size of his father's private member, though it had played a big part in his being here.

'We arrived at Wuthering Heights, I went and opened the door; it was half past six. (Not many doors tell the time.) They had just finished breakfast and were clearing up, wiping porridge off the walls and ceilings. Joseph stood by the hearth poking the fire. It was the only poke he had that year. Hareton was preparing to go to the hayfield.

'"Hur Hur Hur," he laughed, a healthy young onanist.

'"Hello, Nelly," said Heathcliff. He surged forward, reeking of last night's curry. I felt my eyes water. Joseph and Hareton joined him looking at Linton.

'"Surely," said Joseph, "he's swopped wi' ye, master, porridge an' yon' his lass."

'"Speak bloody English, you silly sod," said Heathcliff, shaking the old man by the throat.

'"Hur Hur Hur," said the young onanist.

'Heathcliff stared at his son in an ague of confusion. "Well, have you reared him on snails and sour milk,"[1] he said. "Oh, damn, my soul," he went on, "but that's worse than I expected and the devil knows I was not sanguine."[2] No one knew what he was talking about. Adopting the lotus position on a chair he asked the boy to come hither. The boy hid his face on my shoulder, he then hid it by my elbow, then behind my knee, then under my

[1] A classic Emily Brontë line. *Ed.*
[2] More classic Brontë lines. *Ed.*

foot. Heathcliff pulled him forward. "Do you know who I am ?" he said.

'Linton turned to me and said, "Nelly, this man doesn't know who he is."

'"Hur Hur Hur," went Hareton.

'"Hareton," said Heathcliff, "you infernal calf, begone to your work – such stunning wit is too much."

'So with his infernal calf, Hareton limped away. Meantime, Joseph had brought the boy a bowl of porridge; the boy stirred around the mess. Just his look affirmed he could not eat it. "Can't you see my look? I affirm I cannot eat it," he said.

'"Cannot eat it?" said Joseph.

'"Take it away," said the boy.

'"How far would you like it to go?" interjected Heathcliff.

'The boy hesitated, then said, "Somalia".

'"You heard the boy, Joseph," said Heathcliff. "Take the porridge to Somalia."

'Dutifully Joseph put his hat on and took the porridge to Somalia. Heathcliff stood up and stretched. It was then I saw that terrible swelling in his trousers. I thought, poor little Linton had come through that and lived!

'Having no excuse for lingering longer, Linton was timidly rebuffing the amorous advances of a sheep dog on his leg. So I slipped out. As I closed the door I heard a cry and a frantic repetition of the words, "Don't leave me with this dog screwing my leg, for Christ's sake, don't leave me this way etc, etc."

'Too late – I had ridden off. Even a mile away I could still hear his pitiful etcs.'

Chapter XXI

WE HAD SAD work with Cathy next day. She rose in high glee, eager to see her cousin. Unfortunately the high glee didn't last as he wasn't there. "Where is my cousin?" she cried and cried in that order. Edgar himself tried to soothe and calm Cathy: he put hot bread poultice on her chest, back and forehead, he massaged her legs with warm oil, a hot-water bottle at her feet, ice packs on her head and leeches on her arms. It took her three days to recover . . . during this time her father lay in a happy drunken stupor with four star Martell, a bargain at eighteen shillings. "Linton will schoon come back, and so will I," he predicted.

'I chanced to encounter the housekeeper of Wuthering. She told me Linton was very sickly, always getting coughs, colds, aches and pains as the dog screwed on his leg. I asked how they treated him. She said they put hot bread poultices on his chest and back and forehead. "Did they massage his legs with hot oil?" I asked, "and a hot-water bottle at his feet and leeches on his arms?"

'"Yes," she said.

'"It will take him three days to recover," I said.

'"Did your master get struck twice by lightning?" she asked.

'One day Cathy wished to walk on the moors with the wind and the rain in her hair. "I wish to see if the moor-game have made their nest," she informed me. I put on my bonnet and sallied out; once out, I kept on sallying. She went on ahead, I followed on foot. She bounded before me, like a greyhound. I found plenty to entertain me, listening to the larks singing to the crows cawing, the cuckoos cuckooing, the starlings chattering, the doves cooing, the sparrows chirping and in the *far* distance Joseph on his way to Somalia.

'"Only a little further," said Catherine. "By the time you reach the other side, I shall have raised the bird."[1] I had no idea birds have to be raised, I thought they were happy where they were. "It's only a little farther," said Cathy.

'"You already have a little father," I reminded her.

'Suddenly Heathcliff appeared. "What are you doing on my land?" he said.

'"We're standing on it," said Cathy. "Can't you see?"

'He took us into Wuthering Heights. "You aren't Edgar Linton's daughter, are you?" he asked.

'"Aren't I?" said Cathy. "Then I wonder who I am," she giggled.

'"She's only joking," I explained. "She's Cathy Linton."

'"Ah! your father kills ninety-nine per cent of all known jokes," he said.

'Young Linton stood by the fire. He had been walking in the fields with a junior zimmer. He was waiting for Joseph to come back from Somalia so he could give him more porridge to take back.

'"Now, who is that?" asked Heathcliff of Cathy,

[1] North country meaningless terminology. *Ed.*

prodding the boy with an electric cattle probe.

'"Your son," said Cathy, doing a little pirouette.

'"Yes, he is your cousin," said Heathcliff doing a clog dance.

'"Oh, Linton, my cousin," she said, embracing him with a kiss ten minutes long.

'"That's enough of that," I said, wrenching them apart with a noise like a sink pump.

'"Linton is much better these days," said Heathcliff. "There are periods when he can stand unaided. There are times when he's not fit to be seen and we cover him with a blanket and lock him in the meat-safe."

'"Oh, Linton," Cathy said, clapping her hands and doing a pirouette. "You must come and visit us at the Grange and see our meat-safe."

'"Oh," he groaned. "It's too far for me to walk two miles to see a meat-safe, it would kill me."

'"Only walk one and crawl the rest, you can spread it over a month," she said, doing a pirouette.

'Heathcliff interrupted, "You must know that in the past your father and I quarrelled."

'"Why, oh why?" asked Cathy.

'"He thought me too poor to marry his sister."

'"And, were you poor?"

'"Yes, but I overcame it."

'"How?"

'"We starved."

'"Of course!" said Cathy, suddenly realizing. "You are my uncle, *mon oncle*!" She rushed forward to embrace him, at the last moment he stepped aside and she crashed into a wall. "Why did you do that?" she said.

'"Because," he said, "I am an untouchable."

'"How did your wife embrace you?" said Cathy, puzzled.

'"She wore surgical gloves," said the Untouchable.

'"Linton," he shouted. "Have you nothing to show your cousin anywhere about, not even a rabbit or a weasel's nest?"

'"Oh, how lovely," said Cathy.

'Heathcliff rose, called out of the window for Hareton who was in the fields wanking. When he arrived Heathcliff bid him show Miss Cathy round the stables. "Behave like a gentleman," said Heathcliff. "Don't use bad words like fuck. Keep your hands out of your pockets! Don't *stare*, and when the young lady is looking at you, hide your face."

'Off went Cathy, skipping alongside the oaf. As instructed, he hid his face and walked in a pool, to please Cathy he did it again. She clapped her hands with delight and tripped merrily along seeking objects of amusement like a rabbit and a weasel's nest.

'Hareton took her to see the prize bull. "Hur hur hur," he said. "Will you look at the balls on him."

'Cathy went pale, hid her eyes and backed away saying, "No no no no, how terrible for the poor thing."

'Before we departed Wuthering Heights Heathcliff gave us a cup of curried tea and a poppadom. He waved us goodbye with a Bombay Duck. On the way home, we stopped twice, once to see a rabbit and secondly a weasel's nest. In the distance we could see Joseph on his way back from Somalia. "Why didn't you tell me about my cousin Linton and Uncle Heathcliff?" asked Cathy.

'"It was your father's express wish not to."

'"Express? I wonder why it didn't reach me quicker."

'We arrived back at the Grange to find Master Edgar Linton flat on his back with a bargain at eighteen shillings a bottle. We stood over him.

'"How did you hic get up there, you'll fall off," he said.

'We left him saying, "Get these penguins out of this room!"

'In the morning Master Edgar appeared unsteadily at the top of the stairs. By falling he soon appeared unsteadily at the foot of the stairs. "What happened?" he said.

'"You did," said Cathy.

'While the doctor was stitching his head, and setting his leg, Cathy in high spirits skipped around and sometimes over her father's body.

'"Ah, Cathy," said Master Edgar. "Every day you get more and more like your mother."

'"I hope not," said high-spirited Cathy. "She's dead,"

'"Yes, she's dead," said Master Edgar, bursting into tears; great sobs racked his body. They racked his arms, racked his neck, knees and nose but in between sobs he managed to fit in half a bottle of Tailor's Tawny Port 1804 – it was way past its best, so was he. As we mopped up around him, Cathy merrily asked her father again why he had never ever told her about Linton and Heathcliff. At the mention of the latter, Master Edgar became downcast, but thanks to Famous Grouse he became upcast again.

'"Heathcliff," he snarled, spitting in the fire, missed, hitting the marble surround.

'Against her will Master Edgar, between sips, forbade Cathy to visit Wuthering Heights again and, in between sips – "There's not enough time between sips to get there," she said – he had sips.

'Cathy was heart-broken but she refused a by-pass. But she wrote secretly to Linton. He kept getting pieces of paper with the words secretly on it, "Love Cathy". He sent back pieces of paper with the word "fish". She also wrote love letters that Master Edgar had forbidden."She must stop writing forbidden love letters," he said. On Master Edgar's orders I intercepted all her letters both in- and out-going. I tried to cheer her up, sending her for walks in the torrential rain, then to play hide and seek on her own. On a lead, Master Edgar took her on merry walks through cornfields. To make it more interesting he would sing Psalm 110, accompanied by a fine bottle of Macallan nineteen year old malt whisky available in a half bottle. We really were buggering up her life. We had but one bit of cheer, her father became dangerously ill with bronchitis, he was so drunk it wasn't until he was sober that he knew he'd got it.

'Cathy yearned for him, she lived in a cloud of gloom. One day I found her crying on her knees, then she cried on her shins and ankles. "Oh, fie, silly child," I exclaimed, "you have no real sorrow. Suppose for a minute that master and I were dead."

'"I'd like it to last longer than that," she said, and then with a gesture I had never seen before said, "Oh fie, now piss off."

'Where had she learnt to say "Oh fie, now piss off" from was a mystery. No one, but no one, in the district was a known Piss-Off-sayer. It was a mystery. Should we call the police?

'One afternoon, looking through Cathy's desk, I found a sheaf of love letters from Linton. "Fish", they said. I confronted her with them, "Fish! what does it mean?" I asked.

'"It's a creature that lives in the sea," she said.

'Then I confronted her as I burnt them. Then she confronted me as an evil cow of a woman. Then I confronted her by saying I wasn't. Upstairs the doctor was confronting Master Edgar with his bill and Master Edgar confronted him with his overdraft.

'Under Master's instructions I wrote to Heathcliff telling him that under no circumstances should Linton write "fish" to Miss Cathy. To cheer her up we went for walks in her room. I gazed around for some means of diverting her thoughts. "Look, Miss," I exclaimed excitedly. "A clothes cupboard! — and there's a chest-of drawers and oh! look, a fireplace!" She went into the cupboard and pretended to be an overcoat. In the chest-of-drawers she pretended to be a freshly laundered bed-sheet, then she stood by the fire and pretended to be a scuttle. She was full of gloom.

'"Come," I said cheerily, taking her hands. "Let's run o'er the moor."

'"No," she said. "You bloody well run o'er the moor." It was hard to please him.'[2]

---

[2] Typist error. *Ed.*

Chapter XXII

WE SAUNTERED over the moor, pausing for me to show her a bit of moss, bindweed from a puddle or a broken twig. "What's the matter, girl?" I said. "Don't you like moss or bindweed, look here, you can keep the broken twig."

'At this she burst into tears. "Oh, dear," she sobbed. "What shall I do when you and papa die and I am by myself?"

'"Well, there's flower-arranging or origami and banjo-playing," I said, "and", I added, "your papa and I may not die for years."

'"Can you give me a rough date?" she asked.

'"How about December 1864?" I said.

'"You know, Nelly," she said. "I fret about nothing on earth except papa's illness, I care for nothing in comparison with papa, except eel and mushroom pie with faggots."

'"How dare you think more of eel and mushroom pie with faggots than your father. Your father is ill, but the eel and mushroom pie with faggots is perfectly healthy."

'One evening as we finished our walk, we arrived at a side door to the garden. Cathy danced in front of it while singing "Champagne Charlie is my name". I went round the back to get the key which was on the inside. When I did I heard a horse drawing nigh, the horse then stopped nigh.

'"Who is that?" I whispered through the keyhole as I fumbled for the right key.

'"Ho, Mrs Linton, it's me and my horse," cried a deep voice (for it was he).

'"I shan't speak to you or your horse, Mr Heathcliff" (for it was he), said Cathy.

'"Go away," I said through the keyhole. Heathcliff's horse started a great steaming stream of urination.

'"Let me in, Nelly," said Cathy, "or I'll drown." I let her in. We slammed the door on the deluge, whereforth Heathcliff (for it was he) had to address us through the keyhole. He told us Linton was dying for love of Cathy. He was too weak to even write "Fish"! He'd be under the sod before summer if she did not come and see him. "You'll never get another fish letter."

'"Shoo! Go away," I said.

'"Be it on your head," he said.

'"Be it what on my head?" I asked.'

Chapter XXII

IMPRESSED BY Heathcliff's pleas (for it was he) and his horse (for it was he), on the morrow we journeyed to his home (for it was his). As we approached, a whiff of tandoori hung in the air. We entered the kitchen where Joseph, back from Somalia, sat with a quart of ale, his pipe in his mouth. He was pouring the beer into the bowl and drinking it through the stem. Cathy ran to the hearth to warm herself by the dogs. I asked if the master and his horse were in.

'"Na-ay," snarled Joseph, or rather screamed through his nose, expelling a good half a pound of its contents. Cathy carefully stroked the dog; carefully it bit her.

'"Na-ay," snarled Joseph bringing another half a pound down.

'Then Linton came down in his dressing-gown. "Joseph!" he said in a poorly voice. "My fire has gone out."

'"I know it'll be back soon," said Joseph.

'"Is that you Miss Linton?" said Linton.

'"No, this is me," she said and flew to him, covering him in kisses and embraces and fumbling all the way up to his room where he put his clothes back on.

'"No! you mustn't kiss me," he said, cringeing back in his chair. "Being stripped naked once is enough, maybe same again tomorrow, eh?" Linton had a tiresome cough: eventually even we got tired of it. "You don't despise me, do you Cathy?" he coughed.

'"No," said Cathy. "No, next to papa I love you more than anything except eel and mushroom pie and faggots."

'"Will Heathcliff be away many days?" I asked.

'"Not many," coughed Linton. "He is on the moors, it's the shooting season and he is shooting gamekeepers and farmhands, it helps to keep them down."

'There wasn't much to do so we pulled our chairs around him coughing for an hour. Then he said, "Did you know, your mother loved my father?"

'"Oh, no she didn't," we said.

'"Oh, yes she did!"

'"Oh, no she didn't!"

'"Oh, yes she did."

'"Oh, no she didn't!"

'"Oh, yes she did!"

'It was too much fun for him and he collapsed.

'Cathy was beside herself, so she moved over to where she was, and gave his chair a violent push: it was all in fun. Immediately, the little creep was seized with a life-sapping suffocating cough – it lasted so long we went out for a walk. On our return the fit was over he lay back covered in bronchial spit.

'"How do you feel now, Master Heathcliff?"

'At once the little creep put on a further display of coughing, moaning and retching, plus body convulsions. He kept it up for a quarter of an hour, then he had an interval and we all had tea.

'"I'm sorry I gave your chair a violent push."

'"Pshaw!" he said, "you hurt me so I'll lie awake all night choking with this cough but you won't care, you'll be home warm in bed with eel and mushroom pie with faggots!" He began to wail, "Aeeeeeough! Aweeeeeough! Ohhhhhhhhugh Wareeeeeeeeee Arghhhhhhhmyarse Mie old man said follow the Band!"

'We thanked him for his entertainment and said we were leaving but, before we did, we were recalled by a scream "Oweeoughmyarse" from Linton. We found he had slid from his chair and was lying writhing in his imitation death-throes on the hearth. Unfortunately it had coincided with a fall of soot from the chimney and he lay there black as pitch. We doused him with buckets of water until the white began to show, but all good things come to an end and we took our leave. Even when we were two miles away we could still hear him wailing, "Oh, yes she did."

'"Oh, no she didn't, we replied.

'"Do you like him, Nelly?" asked Cathy.

'"*Like* him?" I gasped. I went on to gasp, "He's the sickliest whining little creep I've ever seen. His father says he'll snuff it before he is twenty!"

'At this my companion waxed serious. "He's younger than I am," she waxed. "I will see him again," she waxed. "By then all the soot will have cleared."

'Suddenly, nothing happened, but it happened suddenly. I told her, "Your intimacy with your cousin must not be revived, even if it means reviving him first."

'"We'll see," was her reply, and she set off at a gallop leaving me to toil in the rear. (Lots of women have toil in their rear, it takes a simple operation to adjust it.) On returning home, I realized I had a chill and was laid up. I was a poor patient, I couldn't even afford a doctor, I thought my illness a calamity only equalled by the

defeat of Napoleon at Waterloo, the Black Hole of
Calcutta or a Southern Railway Restaurant Car.

'Miss Cathy came to wait on me. She waited for three
minutes. Few have slighter reason for complaint than I
had. Among them, Mrs Aida Scraggs from No. 29
Tower Hamlets, London, who had the shits for three
months. My confinement brought me exceedingly low,
so most of the time I was under the bed. Cathy was a
wonderful nurse, like Florence Nighingoon, the Lady
with the Lump. Her days were divided between Master
Edgar and me. The master retired every night at six but
advanced again at seven. I generally needed nothing
after six so I got bugger-all.'

Chapter XXIV

AT THE CLOSE of three weeks, I was able to quit my chamber but the rim left a tell-tale mark on my bottom. I used to spend the evenings in the library, where I asked Cathy to read to me as my eyes were weak. "Then read a weak book," she said jokingly. I could have throttled her. "I know," she said with a sweet smile. I could have throttled her.[1] Suddenly she took all her clothes off and did a frenzied African dance. She had a fanny like a hedgchog. I was too stunned to speak, and she went off to bed. The following night she seemed unsettled. Then smilingly she repeated her rude African dance, flashed her hedgehog, then vanished. No Catherine could I discover, I searched high and low, she must have been between. I listened at Mr Edgar's door, but it was silent save for Grand Armagnac Les Comtesole Cadignan eight years old. I listened to the floors and the walls, but no Cathy, instead a strong smell of oyster, mushroom pie and faggots. I could have throttled her, meanwhile I practised throttling one of the servants, but when he went unconscious the fun went out of it. I extinguished my candle and seated myself at her bed-

---

[1] Totally unnecessary repeat of a sentence. *Ed.*

room window. Then I detected a figure creeping along.
When it emerged into the light I saw it was in fact a
creep.

'The creep was Cathy's groom. Cathy came in and
rode up the stairs, he wearing an hernia belt carried the
horse away. She crapt[2] into the house, when I arose and
confronted her.

'"Where have you been?" I asked.

'"I'll tell you if you promise not to throttle me."

'I nodded till I got tired of doing it.

'"I've been to Wuthering Heights," she said, in such
ecstasy. She rapidly crossed and uncrossed her legs to
ease the tension. "Zillah, his housekeeper, brought us
some warm wine.[3] It was bloody terrible! Linton sat
coughing in his armchair while I swung back and forth
in a rocking-chair. I talked and he coughed away so
merrily.

'"Cough, Linton darling, cough," I said. We planned
where we would go, like Bexhill, and what we would
do in the summer: screw. Linton assured me we were
alone. He told me Joseph was out on his way back to
Somalia with some more porridge and Hareton Earnshaw was out with his dogs in the woods retrieving dead
gamekeepers and farmhands for Heathcliff. It was a
lovely evening. When I went the next time –"

'"You went twice!" I said with horror.

'"Yes, I went there twice but only once," she continued. "As I entered, he was lying on the settee. He half
got up to welcome me, the other half he left on the
settee, but the effort was too much; with a groan and a
fart he fell back. Just then the oaf and wanker, Hareton,

[2] Typing error. *Ed.*
[3] Château Latour, 1840. *Ed.*

burst the door open; he was drunk as a Lord, he was also drunk as a baron and as an admiral. He had been doing the white-eared elephant. He seized Linton by the arm and swung him round his head."

' "Der, get to thy room,' he drooled, throwing Linton into the kitchen. I followed and he shut us out. It was all terrible. *C'était terrible*. I took my leave. I took it with me on my pony. Hareton appeared. 'Der I'm grieved,' he said, 'der, I'm sorry.' So I gave him a cut with my whip. He snatched it and ate it. 'Der, tank you,' he said.' ' "

Chapters XXV, XXVI, XXVII and XXVIII[1]

*L*INTON WROTE to Master Edgar, he begged to see Cathy again. "You inquire after my health, the truth is I haven't any. I am not like my father, I am more your nephew than his son. I am two-thirds nephew and one-third son. I know I have my faults like peeing out of the window at night, but I love Catherine. Yours, Linton. P.S. Fish."

'Finally, Master Edgar, halfway down a bottle of Martell, agreed. Cathy and I rode out to meet Linton and his coughing on the moor. We found him lying on the heath coughing. He did not rise until we were within coughing distance, then he started. He walked so feebly with a stick, he looked so pale I immediately exclaimed. "Christ, Master Heathcliff, how ill you look, why didn't we meet lying down in the hospital?"

'"I'll try and arrange it," he said, and fell back, thud!, and fell asleep with his mouth open. He was awakened by the entry of a fly, and in the ensuing choking he swallowed it.

'"I think," said Cathy, "you'd be more comfortable

[1] That's enough. *Ed.*

at home than sitting here swallowing flies."

'Linton tried to regurgitate the fly, but only brought up a breakfast sausage. We didn't want to leave him lying here for fear people passing by would surely bury him. For safety, we told him to keep coughing.

'"Where are you, you little creep?" came Heathcliff's voice. "Ah, Nelly, can you and Cathy come and have tea with me, please?"

'We hung Linton across a horse, and he coughed us back to Wuthering Heights.

'When we got in, Heathcliff shut the door and locked it. It was a fiendish trap! Heathcliff intended to keep Cathy prisoner and *force* her to marry Linton, which he did.[2] I was kept prisoner in a room. During this period, Heathcliff struck Cathy. "Take that and that and that," he said, each time giving her a curried fish.[3] These were terrible days. *Des journées terribles.* After five days he finally let us go. I'd been bursting to.

'Back at the Grange, Master Edgar was on his last legs, he only had one pair left. He could barely manage Crofts Original 1793. I sat by his bed, I sat by his cupboard, I sat by his chest-of-drawers, but no matter where I sat, he still went on dying.

'There was a rapid knocking on the door. It made me jump, I reached four feet eight inches. An alkomer's record for my age. It was Cathy! "Is papa still alive?" she asked.

'"Yes, yes," I said. "Hurry up, he's waiting to die." She arrived at his bedside to see a bottle of £1/10s. slip from his nerveless fingers.

2 An old Asian custom. *Ed.*
3 Very quick marriage. *Ed.*

'Cathy sat by his bed all night but, exhausted, she fell asleep, during which time he snuffed it, so she missed him. Yes he had gone, so had the £1/10s.

'The funeral was hurried, the coffin was dropped in the hole and in ten minutes it was filled in. It was a sad day, *une journée triste.*'

Chapters XXIX and XXX

FTER THE funeral, Cathy and I were seated in the library when Heathcliff was admitted. Time had little altered his person, it was still as big as ever. Cathy went to dash from his presence.

'"Stop," he said, arresting her by his arm. "I'm arresting you by your arm," he continued. "I've come to take you home to Wuthering Heights and your husband. Make haste."

'He faced the fire and said, "The day Catherine was buried, I stood by the grave. I realized that two yards of loose earth was all that lay between us. I got a spade and got down to the coffin. I split the lid and I thought I'll have her in my arms yet. If she be cold, I'll get a hot-water bottle. I lifted the lid and there lay my Cathy, her face had gone a bit."

'I interrupted him, "Mr Heathcliff, how can you disturb the dead!"

'"It's very easy," he said. "All you need is a shovel."

'Cathy came down, packed with make haste. "Good-bye, Nelly," said she, her lips like ice. "Come and see me."

'So there and then I went and saw her. Joseph held the front door in his hand. When he let go, it fell off and he

was off to Somalia again. Heathcliff forebade me to see
Cathy, handing me a blindfold.

'But in the village I met Zillah. She told me how
Cathy used to come downstairs to say that her husband
and his cough were very ill. "We know that," Heathcliff
had told her. "His life is not worth a farthing." "Non-
sense," Cathy had told him. "A good loss adjuster
quoted his value as ten pounds." "Ha, ha," Heathcliff
had retorted. "Hur, Hur Hur," Hareton had echoed.
"No one cares what becomes of him." "I'll tell you
what will become of him," Cathy had said. "A corpse!"
"Hur Hur Hur," Hareton had scoffed.

'Zillah went on, "I don't know how Linton and
Cathy managed together, I think she managed together
and he managed together. He and his cough managed
together all night. She never got any rest. It was the
honeymoon and he never stopped only to cough. You'd
find her asleep in the bath, on top of the cupboard, in a
tree, anywhere to get away from him. One night,
shattered by shagging she came to my chamber. 'Tell
Mr Heathcliff his son has stopped doing it and is dying.'
I delivered the message. He took a candle to Linton's
room, setting the curtains alight. Cathy sat by the bed,
her hands folded over her knees. 'He's dead,' said Heathcliff. Cathy, nearly deranged, lifted up her night gown.
'I know,' she said. 'Look what he's missing.' So Heathcliff looked at what he was missing. I gave Cathy some
wine, Château Latour 1839, a very good year. It was a
full-bodied claret, with plenty of fruit and acidity, ma-
tured in oak casks. Joseph carried the stiff into another
room. He was going to take him to Somalia till we
stopped him. Cathy remained by herself, *toute seule*.[1] In
the morning we told Cathy to come down from her

1 French for alone. *Ed.*

tree for breakfast. She arrived down and fell asleep in the porridge. Joseph stood by to take it to Somalia. 'Der, sum one's bin sleeping in my porridge,' said Hareton.''

'Next day they buried Linton, he wouldn't keep any longer. The priest sprinkled cough mixture on his coffin.

'"Onc Sunday evening," Zillah continued, "Cathy came down to the kitchen. She wore black (noir[2]). 'I see you are wearing black noir,' I said to her. 'Joseph and I generally go the Chapel of a Sunday.' 'Then bloody well go to chapel,' she said. Then Hareton came in to give her his company, a pity his company had just gone bankrupt. As she read a haddock-stretching manual by the fire, the oaf crept up behind her and stroked her hair. Cathy recoiled with fury, he recoiled without it. 'How dare you touch me. If you dare come near me I'll go out somewhere else like Lee-on-Sea.' 'I'm zorry,' said the oaf. 'That's no good,' she snapped. 'Go to bloody chapel!'"'

'I myself was shocked at what I had heard. Time and again I tried to gain ingress into Wuthering Heights, but failed, so I waited.'

[2] A black noir. Ed.

Envoi

*T*HUS ENDED Mrs Nelly Dean's story to me. She asked for it in cash. Notwithstanding the doctor, I am rapidly recovering strength. I can sit up and cough and play the banjo on my own soon. I propose getting on horseback and coughing there in memory of Linton. I went to the Heights bearing a note from Mrs Dean to Cathy.

The front door was open, but the jealous gate[1] was fastened. I knocked and Hareton came and unchained the gate. It took him two hours, but he does his best, apparently, to make the least of his advantages. Was Heathcliff at home? No. I announced I would come in and wait. At this Hareton dropped his shovel full of shit and accompanied me in. We entered together so got jammed in the doorway. Cathy was there preparing eel and mushroom pie and chips for the approaching meal. I looked in all directions but couldn't see a meal approaching. Cathy hardly raised her eyes to notice me, even though I ahem'ed several times. I dismounted my horse and had him led away. She did not return my bow, but Hareton said, pointing at me, 'Hur hur, look at him.'

[1] A Brontëism. *Ed.*

At an appropriate moment, I dropped Mrs Dean's note on Cathy's knee.

She asked aloud, 'What's that?'

'A knee,' I said, and she knocked it off. It had been some time since she had knocked it off. 'It's a letter from your housekeeper,' I informed her.

She went to seize it, but Hareton got it first, he put it in his waistcoat pocket, then his breast pocket, then his hip pocket, his trouser pocket, then into his sock, down his trouser front, then under his hat. That done, he gave it back to her. She perused the letter eagerly, then eagerly she threw it in the fire. Then Hareton took a watering-can and went to water the horses. He came back, he walked moodily in, his eyes fixed on the floor; he tripped arse over tip. From the horizontal position he said, 'Der – what brought you here?'

'Ah, an idle whim,' I said.

'Ah, an idle whim?' said Heathcliff.

'I often have them. I had idle whims this morning, my mother had whims very badly, the last one killed her, she had a whim to jump off Beachy Head.'

He then said, 'Stay to dinner, Catherine will prepare a meal.' She appeared with a tray of knives and forks. 'That's no bloody good,' he said. 'We want some food!' With Heathcliff on one hand and Hareton on the other, my arms were trapped. I had to eat like a pig at the trough. That evening I rode home, having dined on eel and oyster vindaloo. All night long I had the shits, so ends the romance of Wuthering Heights.

MANY YEARS later, one day I was out riding and a sudden impulse seized me, just behind the knee. I wished to visit Wuthering Heights. I asked a villager how far it was. 'Fourteen miles as the crow flies,' he said. I told him I was not travelling by crow and set off. Very warm streams of perspiration ran down my body,through my underpants, down my legs and into my boots, where it escaped through the lace–holes as steam.

I could smell the fragrance of stocks with just a hint of horse shit. Through the hall I could see Hareton and Cathy. They were together. I was together but I was on my own. Cathy was teaching Hareton reading.

'Der,' he read, 'Der quick brown fox jumps over the lazy dog.'

'Very good,' said Cathy, and as a reward she kissed him and he gave her boobs a quick squeeze.

Then Mrs Nelly Dean spotted me. 'Mr Lockwood, what are you doing here?'

'Ah, Nelly Dean, do you know, there's an old mill by the stream?' I told her I'd come to pay Heathcliff the rent.

'Haven't you heard?' she said.

I listened but I couldn't hear anything. She told me that Zillah had left and now she was housekeeper. I could hear that. She also told me that Cathy and Hareton were in love. 'Have a drink, you must be weary.'

'Yes,' I said. 'Ah gits weary and sick of tryin'. I'm tired of libbin' but 'feard o' dying . . . dat old man ribber he just keeps rolling a long.'

'Oh, I am sorry,' she said, 'Mr Heathcliff has passed on.'

Quickly I put the money away. 'How did he die?' I asked.

'Well, he started taking walks at night in the wind and the rain. He used to come back flooded, and we had to empty him out. "She's out there!" he'd say, pointing out — some nights he got it wrong and pointed in. One night I went to his room to bid him goodnight, but he had gone. I looked in his bed, he was gone. I looked

under the bed, gone. I looked in his suits, there was
nobody in them or money. I thought, is it a ghost or a
vampire? One night he was on the moor in a lightning
storm and I clearly heard him call, "Cathy, my love,
come and look at this!" When he came back at dawn he
was black, smouldering his eyebrows and his clothes
were scorched. He had been struck by lightning twice in
the same place.[2] He went up to his room. Then came
that final night. At dusk he went into his chamber. All
night long he was moaning "Cathy, my love." Joseph
shouted out, "Stop that fucking noise, it's worse than
Somalia." It was terrible. In the morning I tapped on his
door and went in with his breakfast and there was Mr
Heathcliff.

'Where?' I said.

'There,' she said. 'I could not think him dead, but the
way he looked I couldn't think of him alive either.'

'But you had a choice of two?' I said helpfully.

'Just in case he was dead I ate his breakfast.'

'He was perfectly still,' she continued.

'Oh, that's a sign of death,' I said helpfully.

'He and the bed were soaking wet, a water main over
his head had burst in the night,' said Mrs Dean.

'Was he drowned in his sleep?' I asked helpfully.

'It's hard to say,' she said.

'No, it isn't. I just said it, and I didn't find it hard,' I
said helpfully.

'I, I,' stammered Mrs Dean, overcome by overcome-
ness. 'I touched his body, it were ice cold so I knew he'd
keep a bit, I could doubt no more, Mr Lockwood. He
was dead, and I sobbed in grief. The bastard hadn't paid
me for three months. Old Joseph came in the room, he

[2] A coincidence. *Ed*.

knelt and crossed himself. Why not? He'd crossed every-
thing else. We tried to close Heathcliff's eyes but they
wouldn't, so with the aid of pliers we glued them. Poor
Hareton sat by the corpse all night, it was no use: in the
morning it was still there. The autopsy said he had died
from African swamp fever that had affected his
swonnicles.

'To celebrate after the funeral Hareton married Cathy;
they were the perfect mismatch.'

So ended the story of Wuthering Heights, except for
one occasion, I was riding on the moors when I saw a
shepherd boy and his sheep. He was trembling. He
hadn't been paid for three months.

'What ails thee, lad?' I asked.

'There's Heathcliff, and a woman yonder,' he said,
and they're doing it.'

THE END

READ MORE IN PENGUIN

In every corner of the world, on every subject under the sun, Penguin represents quality and variety – the very best in publishing today.

For complete information about books available from Penguin – including Puffins, Penguin Classics and Arkana – and how to order them, write to us at the appropriate address below. Please note that for copyright reasons the selection of books varies from country to country.

In the United Kingdom: Please write to *Dept. JC, Penguin Books Ltd, FREEPOST, West Drayton, Middlesex UB7 0BR.*

If you have any difficulty in obtaining a title, please send your order with the correct money, plus ten per cent for postage and packaging, to *PO Box No. 11, West Drayton, Middlesex UB7 0BR*

In the United States: Please write to *Consumer Sales, Penguin USA, P.O. Box 999, Dept. 17109, Bergenfield, New Jersey 07621-0120.* VISA and MasterCard holders call 1-800-253-6476 to order all Penguin titles

In Canada: Please write to *Penguin Books Canada Ltd, 10 Alcorn Avenue, Suite 300, Toronto, Ontario M4V 3B2*

In Australia: Please write to *Penguin Books Australia Ltd, P.O. Box 257, Ringwood, Victoria 3134*

In New Zealand: Please write to *Penguin Books (NZ) Ltd, Private Bag 102902, North Shore Mail Centre, Auckland 10*

In India: Please write to *Penguin Books India Pvt Ltd, 706 Eros Apartments, 56 Nehru Place, New Delhi 110 019*

In the Netherlands: Please write to *Penguin Books Netherlands bv, Postbus 3507, NL-1001 AH Amsterdam*

In Germany: Please write to *Penguin Books Deutschland GmbH, Metzlerstrasse 26, 60594 Frankfurt am Main*

In Spain: Please write to *Penguin Books S. A., Bravo Murillo 19, 1° B, 28015 Madrid*

In Italy: Please write to *Penguin Italia s.r.l., Via Felice Casati 20, I-20124 Milano*

In France: Please write to *Penguin France S. A., 17 rue Lejeune, F-31000 Toulouse*

In Japan: Please write to *Penguin Books Japan, Ishikiribashi Building, 2-5-4, Suido, Bunkyo-ku, Tokyo 112*

In Greece: Please write to *Penguin Hellas Ltd, Dimocritou 3, GR-106 71 Athens*

In South Africa: Please write to *Longman Penguin Southern Africa (Pty) Ltd, Private Bag X08, Bertsham 2013*

BY THE SAME AUTHOR

A Selection

Lady Chatterley's Lover According to Spike Milligan

In Spike Milligan's intense, steaming, palpitating, lustful, unexpurgated retelling of Lady Chatterley's romps with a member of the lower orders (with footnotes), many hitherto unknown aspects are revealed (as well as – all too frequently – the gamekeeper's delicate white loins).

Perhaps the reader may not have been aware of Sir Clifford Chatterley's penchant for stretched haddock, or that Mellors had a fetish for collecting toenail clippings? Certainly, readers will pick up a multiplicity of tips on flower-arranging and where to put their creeping-jenny. Which brings us back to Mellors's delicate white loins ...

The Bible According to Spike Milligan

There have been many versions of the Old Testament over the centuries but never one quite like this. Spike Milligan has rewritten, in his own inimitable style, many of the best-known stories of the Old Testament, featuring characters like King (my brain hurts) Solomon, the great oar of a giant Goliath and the well-known *Telegraph* crossword clue Hushai the Archite. Believers and non-believers alike will enjoy this hilarious re-working, where the jokes, jests and jibes tumble over each other from Chapter One, Verse One until the end.

Adolf Hitler: My Part in His Downfall

Bathos, pathos, gales of drunken laughter, and insane military goonery explode in superlative Milliganese.

Mussolini: My Part in His Downfall

Britannia rules the waves, but sometimes she waives the rules, and Spike is set to liberate – *gasp* – Italy.

Peace Work

It's 1946 and Spike, newly demobbed, goes on tour all over Britain and parts of Europe. Then he teams up with Harry Secombe, Michael Bentine and Peter Sellers. They became 'The Goons'. The rest is history.